I to I

I to I

A Personal Post-Eschatology

LOUIS IGOU HODGES

RESOURCE *Publications* • Eugene, Oregon

I TO I
A Personal Post-Eschatology

Copyright © 2009 Louis Igou Hodges. All rights reserved. Except for brief quotations in critical publications or reviews, no part of this book may be reproduced in any manner without prior written permission from the publisher. Write: Permissions, Wipf and Stock, 199 W. 8th Ave., Suite 3, Eugene, OR 97401.

Resource Publications
A division of Wipf and Stock Publishers
199 W. 8th Ave., Suite 3
Eugene, OR 97401

www.wipfandstock.com

ISBN 13: 978-1-60608-082-5

Manufactured in the U.S.A.

New Revised Standard Version Bible, © 1989, Division of Christian Education of the National Council of the Churches of Christ in the United States of America. Used by permission. All rights reserved.

Contents

1. Introduction • 1
2. Foretastes of Heaven Experienced on the Earth • 10
3. Seeing the Lord • 18
4. The Judgment Seat of Christ • 30
5. The Promises of God Fulfilled • 45
6. The Heavenly Environment • 60
7. The Personal Dimension • 73
8. The Social Relationships • 91
9. Activities Here • 99
10. Implications for the Mortal Life • 106

I

Introduction

Eternity

Dear _____,

I am you. I am definitely you in every sense. I am your personality, your body, your consciousness, and I have all of your memories. I know the innermost secrets of your heart, your feelings, your disappointments, and your joys. But I am not you. In fact, I am quite different from you. How can I be both you and not you? The answer is that I am the transformed, glorified you now made like Christ in His resurrected and ascended state. I live in the new world that is not cursed, but blessed, a world without temptation, opposition, or enemies, a world without deterioration, danger, or uncertainty.

Through an extraordinary providential permission I am being allowed to communicate with you during your mortal existence in time from the depths of eternity, far beyond the confines of what the glorified inhabitants call the former heavens and earth. This communication is possible because the God we worship exists outside the boundaries of all temporal confinement. In fact all of His communications are from a depth, transcending all space and time, that even glorified saints and the angelic hosts cannot fathom. We will never be able to venture where He is and always has been in His unique transcendence and aseity (the quality of God's being by which He contains the ground of His existence within Himself, in contrast with every created thing which is brought into being by One outside itself and is therefore dependent by its very nature).

I hope that these words will cause you to think more profoundly and seriously about heaven since it is my/your eternal abode. I remember how little teaching and how few sermons I heard on this subject during my vapor-length existence in the former world. However, Scripture indicates that a proper view of the future, which God has for His people, puts all of the mortal life in the right focus. James powerfully proclaims that life in the mortal sphere is just a mist which vanishes away quickly when compared with eternity.[1] The Psalmist wrote concerning godless people, "But when I thought how to understand this, it seemed to me a wearisome task, until I went into the sanctuary of God; then I perceived their end."[2] For the apostle Paul, the resurrection of Jesus Christ is important not only because it validates the truth of the Gospel, but also because it points decisively to that great climax and the end of history in which Christ will triumph finally and decisively over all the enemies of God.[3]

---

1. Jas 4:14—"Yet you do not even know what tomorrow will bring. What is your life? For you are a mist that appears for a little while and then vanishes."

2. Ps 73:16–17.

3. 1 Cor 15:12–29—"Now if Christ is proclaimed as raised from the dead, how can some of you say there is no resurrection of the dead? If there is no resurrection of the dead, then Christ has not been raised; and if Christ has not been raised, then our proclamation has been in vain and your faith has been in vain. We are even found to be misrepresenting God, because we testified of God that he raised ChristCwhom he did not raise if it is true that the dead are not raised. For if the dead are not raised, then Christ has not been raised. If Christ has not been raised, your faith is futile and you are still in your sins. Then those also who have died in Christ have perished. If for this life only we have hoped in Christ, we are of all people most to be pitied. But in fact Christ has been raised from the dead, the first fruits of those who have died. For since

In these communications I have been prohibited from going beyond what God's eternal written Word ("The Lord exists forever; your word is firmly fixed in heaven"[4]) declares in the same way that Paul was not allowed to recount the inexpressible words which he witnessed when he ascended into the third heaven.[5] It is both foolish and presumptuous for any created being to seek to know what God does not intend for us to know or to know it before His perfect time. I am permitted, however, to point out clear implications of the sacred text. The omniscient God has provided in His Word all that is necessary for life and godliness in your world[6]; His inspired (that is, "God-breathed")

---

death came through a human being, the resurrection of the dead has also come through a human being; for as all die in "Adam, so all will be made alive in Christ. But each in his own order: Christ the first fruits, then at his coming those who belong to Christ. Then comes the end, when he hands over the kingdom to God the Father, after he has destroyed every ruler and every authority and power. For he must reign until he has put all his enemies under his feet. The last enemy to be destroyed is death. For 'God has put all things in subjection under his feet.' But when it says, 'All things are put in subjection,' it is plain that this does not include the one who put all things in subjection under him. When all things are subjected to him, then the Son himself will also be subjected to the one who put all things in subjection under him, so that God may be all in all. Otherwise, what will those people do who receive baptism on behalf of the dead? If the dead are not raised at all, why are people baptized on their behalf?"

4. Ps 119:89.

5. 2 Cor 12:2–4—"I know a person in Christ who fourteen years ago was caught up to the third heaven—whether in the body or out of the body I do not know; God knows. And I know that such a person—whether in the body or out of the body I do not know; God knows—was caught up into Paradise and heard things that are not to be told, that no mortal is permitted to repeat."

6. 2 Pet 1:3—"His divine power has given us everything needed for life and godliness, through the knowledge of him who called us by his own glory and goodness."

Word is profitable for teaching (it put forth what God's children ought to believe), for reproof (it warned God's children of false teaching which had to be rejected), for correction (it warned of practices and conduct which brought God's judgment), and for training in righteousness (it put forth the conduct and attitudes which brought God's favor).[7] It is His Word that needed to be used to correct the speculation and erroneous ideas which kept circulating in the former world concerning heaven. Scripture was the only reliable source, the final authority on such matters. Anecdotal reports of near-death experiences, claims of false religions, and poetic imaginations must not be allowed to dim or replace the light of God's sure Word.

My experiences in this new world have enabled me better to understand the limitations on human language which Biblical authors faced in articulating their prophecies and occasional visions of heaven. In fact I am struggling to express my thoughts within what I now realize were incredibly narrow linguistic boundaries imposed by the structure of the language which I used in the former life and the terrestrial dimensions under which I lived. Our vocabulary and our thought forms have been graciously elevated to previously unimaginable heights in the new universe because of our glorified state, our closer relationship with God, our great preoccupation with His worship and adoration, and the fact that we are one with the whole body of Christ, all operating with the one great agenda of knowing, serving, and worshiping the Triune God. Those who have experienced such a holy unity, beyond all earthly comprehension, often do not need words to communicate. Our thoughts proceed from such a loftier mental and spiritual framework that even the

---

7. 2 Tim 3:16–17—"All scripture is inspired by God and is useful for teaching, for reproof, for correction, and for training in righteousness, so that everyone who belongs to God may be proficient, equipped for every good work."

loftiest conceptual grids of the former life seem so infantile and base in comparison (how merciful God was to bear with us in that former state). There will be times in these communications when no earthly vocabulary will even closely approximate the reality behind the heavenly word so that only a feeble approximation can be attempted.

In Scripture "heaven" is used in speaking of three different realms. (1) It refers to the atmospheric heaven (the aerial) where the birds soar and the highest mountains penetrate,[8] (2) the stellar heaven (the sidereal) or the physical universe which includes the stars, galaxies and constellations,[9] and (3) the third heaven (the celestial, the heaven of heavens) which is God's abode.[10] God is most certainly immense (in Himself) and omnipresent (in relation to the created order). Solomon affirms in His great prayer of dedication, "But will God indeed dwell on the earth? Even heaven and the highest heaven cannot contain you, much less this house that I have built!"[11] In a similar manner the Psalmist (David according to the Psalm title) addressed God with these words:

> Where can I go from your spirit? Or where can I flee from your presence?
> If I ascend to heaven, you are there; if I make my bed in Sheol, you are there.
> If I take the wings of the morning and settle at the farthest limits of the sea,

---

8. Deut 28:12—"The Lord will open for you his rich storehouse, the heavens, to give the rain of your land in its season and to bless all your undertakings. You will lend to many nations, but you will not borrow."

9. Heb 1:10—"In the beginning, Lord, you founded the earth, and the heavens are the work of your hands. . . ."

10. 2 Cor 12:2–4—see note 5.

11. 1 Kgs 8:27.

> Even there your hand shall lead me, and your right hand shall hold me fast.
>
> If I say, 'Surely the darkness shall cover me, and the light around me become night,'
>
> Even the darkness is not dark to you; the night is as bright as the day, for darkness is as light to you.[12]

Such passages make it clear that God is present in the totality of His being at all points in the universe. However, (the third) heaven is the place where His glory is especially present, where He communicates with and commands the angelic hosts (it is His throne), and where He dwells in special relationship with the redeemed body of Christ. Isaiah prays, "Look down from heaven and see, from your holy and glorious habitation. Where are your zeal and your might? The yearning of your heart and your compassion? They are withheld from me."[13] Isaiah also states concerning God, "Heaven is my throne and the earth is my footstool; what is the house that you would build for me, and what is my resting place?"[14] In a similar manner, the author of Hebrews affirms, "But you have come to Mount Zion and to the city of the living God, the heavenly Jerusalem, and to innumerable angels in festal gathering, and to the assembly of the firstborn who are enrolled in heaven, and to God the judge of all, and to the spirits of the righteous made perfect. . . ."[15] Heaven is the place where God is said to have His sanctuary (where He is worshiped by the angels and the redeemed[16]) and

12. Ps 139:7–12.

13. Isa 63:15.

14. Isa 66:1.

15. Heb 12:22–23.

16. Rev 5:11–14—"Then I looked, and I heard the voice of many angels surrounding the throne and the living creatures and the elders; they

His habitation, a place of holiness,[17] and great beauty (the city has gates of pearls, is of pure gold like clear glass with precious foundation stones).[18] It is also a place of unfathomable exhilaration. The Psalmist wrote, "You show me the path of life. In your presence there is fullness of joy; in your right hand are pleasures forevermore."[19] It is the place where the joy of Christ is shared with those who remained loyal to Him in the midst of earthly trials,[20] those who were martyred for Him,[21] and those who overcame the corrupting influences of the world, the devil, and the flesh.[22]

---

numbered myriads of myriads and thousands of thousands, singing with full voice, 'Worthy is the Lamb that was slaughtered to receive power and wealth and wisdom and might and honor and glory and blessing!' Then I heard every creature in heaven and on earth and under the earth and in the sea, and all that is in them, singing, 'To the one seated on the throne and to the Lamb be blessing and honor and glory and might forever and ever!' And the four living creatures said, 'Amen!' And the elders fell down and worshiped."

17. Rev 21:27—"But nothing unclean will enter it, nor anyone who practices abomination or falsehood, but only those who are written in the Lamb's book of life."

18. Rev 21:11–21.

19. Ps 16:11.

20. Luke 22:28–30—"You are those who have stood by me in my trials; and I confer on you, just as my Father has conferred on me, a kingdom, so that you may eat and drink at my table in my kingdom, and you will sit on thrones judging the twelve tribes of Israel."

21. Rev 20:4—"Then I saw thrones, and those seated on them were given authority to judge. I also saw the souls of those who had been beheaded for their testimony to Jesus and for the word of God. They had not worshiped the beast or its image and had not received its mark on their foreheads or their hands. They came to life and reigned with Christ a thousand years."

22. Rev 2:26—"To everyone who conquers and continues to do my works to the end, I will give authority over the nations. . . ." Rev

Heaven is rightly described both as a state and a place. It is a state in that it symbolizes intimate knowledge of the Triune God and unending, conscious fellowship with Him. It is a place in that it is substantial; it has essence or substance. It is not merely a state of the mind or some kind of psychological reality. Neither is it merely a place for spirits. It is the place where Jesus ascended in His resurrection body and where we glorified saints now abide in a literal, physical existence. John wrote,

> Then I saw a new heaven and a new earth; for the first heaven and the first earth had passed away, and the sea was no more. And I saw the holy city, the new Jerusalem, coming down out of heaven from God, prepared as a bride adorned for her husband. And I heard a loud voice from the throne saying, "See, the home of God is among mortals. He will dwell with them as their God; they will be his peoples, and God himself will be with them. . . ."[23]

In fact it is more real than the former heavens and the earth, which passed away with a great roar and were dissolved with fervent heat as all of the works of the former world were burned up[24]; it will never be destroyed; its foundations are eternally stable and sure.[25] The real existence of heaven thunders in testi-

---

3:21—"To the one who conquers I will give a place with me on my throne, just as I myself conquered and sat down with my Father on his throne."

23. Rev 21:1–3.

24. 2 Pet 3:10.

25. Isa 66:22—"For as the new heavens and the new earth, which I will make, shall remain before me, says the Lord; so shall your descendants and your name remain."

mony to the truthfulness of God's statement, "[F]or what can be seen is temporary, but what cannot be seen is eternal."[26]

The reality of heaven ought to call each person in the mortal life to a type of self-transcendence. The future abode in God's presence means that life's meaning and purpose issue from Him, the Creator and Redeemer, not from the creature or the created world. It means that the mortal life is incomplete and will reach its completion and fulfillment only as God Himself brings His creative and redemptive program to its consummation in the new heavens and the new earth. Seeking meaning and fulfillment outside the Creator leads only to frustration, disappointment, and futility. But we the glorified are experiencing now the wonder of fulfillment, of meaning, and of purpose in the intimate relationship with God through Jesus Christ in its consummated stage.

It is thrilling being able to communicate with you from this glorious vantage point. I hope that my comments will assist you in your earthly pilgrimage and increase your joy as you are in the journey toward what we became millions of earth years ago.

---

26. 2 Cor 4:18.

2

Foretastes of Heaven Experienced on the Earth

Eternity

Dear ,

There is a sense in which the blessings in which we now are immersed, are not totally new. God in His grace gave us anticipations of these blessings in the mortal life. Still while in the former existence we saw and understood the things of God so obliquely and imperfectly; we saw in a mirror dimly but now we see face to face; we knew in part, but now we know fully as we were known.[1] What God revealed was absolutely true because God's word was and is truth,[2] but our capacity—limited by our finiteness, our earthbound condition, and especially our depravity—could only absorb a spoonful of God's ocean of truth. God declared, "For my thoughts are not your thoughts, nor are your ways my ways, says the Lord. For as the heavens are higher than the earth, so are my ways higher than your ways and my thoughts than your thoughts."[3]

Yet, in ways which we only faintly perceived, God enabled us to begin to enter into and to experience the ultimate blessings

---

1. 1 Cor 13:12—"For now we see in a mirror, dimly, but then we will see face to face. Now I know only in part; then I will know fully, even as I have been fully known."

2. John 17:17—"Sanctify them in the truth; your word is truth."

3. Isa 55:8–9.

of eternity within that former existence. We were told (1) that we had eternal life, that our experience of eternal life had already commenced. Jesus had said, "Very truly, I tell you, anyone who hears my word and believes him who sent me has eternal life, and does not come under judgment, but has passed from death to life."[4] Scripture also stated (2) that we were seated with Christ in the heavenly places,[5] and that (3) we had already come to the city of the living God.[6] Indeed eternal life had already begun, and we had surrendered ourselves to live under the dominion of the King of Heaven and to live as His obedient subjects. Through Christ's work as our Great High Priest we were able by faith to enter into the ultimate "Holy of Holies," the very presence of God, the access to which was symbolized by the tearing of the veil of the temple at the moment of Christ's death.[7] We were able to enter into God's presence with confidence[8] and

---

4. John 5:24. This truth that we had already entered into eternal life was what theologians of that older order called "realized eschatology" as opposed to future eschatology.

5. Eph 2:4–6—"But God, who is rich in mercy, out of the great love with which he loved us even when we were dead through our trespasses, made us alive together with Christ—by grace you have been saved—and raised us up with him and seated us with him in the heavenly places in Christ Jesus. . . ."

6. Heb 12:22–23.

7. Matt 27:5–51—"Then Jesus cried again with a loud voice and breathed his last. At that moment the curtain of the temple was torn in two, from top to bottom. The earth shook, and the rocks were split."

8. Heb 4:14–16—"Since, then, we have a great high priest who has passed through the heavens, Jesus, the Son of God, let us hold fast to our confession. For we do not have a high priest who is unable to sympathize with our weaknesses, but we have one who in every respect has been tested as we are, yet without sin. Let us therefore approach the throne of grace with boldness, so that we may receive mercy and find grace to help in time of need."

boldness.⁹ This entrance was a foretaste of our entrance into the final heaven and the eternal rest prepared for us. The Holy Spirit had produced longings and aspirations for greater fellowship with God which were a blessed anticipation of the sweetness of heavenly communion.¹⁰

God graciously gave us the Holy Spirit to dwell within us. The Spirit served as down payment or pledge of the heavenly inheritance which we are now enjoying.¹¹ He was God's first installment of the promised blessings. The Spirit was the seal (pointing to the absolute certainty) of the great future God had for us.¹² In the communion with the indwelling Spirit we had marvelous foretastes of the eternal communion which we are now enjoying with God. Jesus said, "[F]or I tell you that from now on I will not drink of the fruit of the vine until the kingdom of God comes."¹³ The Spirit's prompting, encouraging, leading,

---

9. Heb 10:19–22—"Therefore, my friends, since we have confidence to enter the sanctuary by the blood of Jesus, by the new and living way that he opened for us through the curtain (that is, through his flesh), and since we have a great priest over the house of God, let us approach with a true heart in full assurance of faith, with our hearts sprinkled clean from an evil conscience and our bodies washed with pure water."

10. Phil 3:10–11—"I want to know Christ and the power of his resurrection and the sharing of his sufferings by becoming like him in his death, if somehow I may attain the resurrection from the dead." Phil 1:23—"I am hard pressed between the two: my desire is to depart and be with Christ, for that is far better. . . ."

11. Eph 1:13–14—"In him you also, when you had heard the word of truth, the gospel of your salvation, and had believed in him, were marked with the seal of the promised Holy Spirit; this is the pledge of our inheritance towards redemption as God's own people, to the praise of his glory."

12. 1 Cor 1:22—"[B]y putting his seal on us and giving us his Spirit in our hearts as a first installment." 2 Cor 5:5—"He who has prepared us for this very thing is God, who has given us the Spirit as a guarantee."

13. Luke 22:18.

and enlightening all pointed to the much deeper and more intense fellowship with God which is ours in the final estate.

We believers had the first fruits of the Spirit, causing us to groan (that is to long with deep desire for the future consummation and to be dissatisfied under the conditions of the curse), waiting for our adoption as sons at the redemption of the body.[14] Christ's resurrection was the first fruits of those who die in Him.[15] His resurrection made the experience of eternal life absolute and sure and proved conclusively that in the new earth we would be in our same bodies, not just in a spiritual or ghostly form. Furthermore, believers were called the first fruits among God's creatures.[16] God so planned that through our lives in the mortal sphere the rays of eternity would shine, that through our conduct, conversation, and attitudes, the gleams of eternity might break through. In fact, when we were born again we experienced a new creation and became in our spirits part of the new heavens and the new earth so that the evil world around us was no longer our true home.[17] Believers reflected eternity not in the sense that

14. Rom 8:23—"[A]nd not only the creation, but we ourselves, who have the first fruits of the Spirit, groan inwardly while we wait for adoption, the redemption of our bodies."

15. 1 Cor 15:20–23—"But in fact Christ has been raised from the dead, the first fruits of those who have died. For since death came through a human being, the resurrection of the dead has also come through a human being; for as all die in Adam, so all will be made alive in Christ. But each in his own order: Christ the first fruits, then at his coming those who belong to Christ."

16. Jas 1:18—In fulfilment of his own purpose he gave us birth by the word of truth, so that we would become a kind of first fruits of his creatures."

17. 2 Cor 5:17—"So if anyone is in Christ, there is a new creation: everything old has passed away; see, everything has become new!" The very vocabulary used for the original creation and for the new heavens and the new earth were used of the recreation which took place when one was incorporated into Christ.

they were exempt from all suffering, trial, and difficulties, but in their love for God, the example of a holy walk, the testimony of self-giving love toward others, and perseverance under setbacks and persecution. Obedience, godliness, and holiness pointed to the values and to the very life of heaven. The kingdom of God was made manifest in His kingly rule in the mortal lives of His subjects as it is now made perfectly and absolutely manifest in heaven.[18] The hope of eternity in God's presence was very much a purifying element for believers in the mortal sphere.[19]

When we first exercised faith in Jesus Christ we became citizens of heaven with all the rights involved in that citizenship.[20] It is as though heaven was in us before we ever came here. By faith that border into eternity was crossed in the mortal life. We were exhorted to live in the former world as citizens of heaven and to become increasingly what we already were in Christ. Though physically and mentally we still existed in the former world, we had a real spiritual existence in the age to come[21]; in fact our real sense of belonging, our truest identity,

---

18. Jesus taught His disciples to pray, "Your kingdom come. Your will be done, on earth as it is in heaven." (Matt 6:10). Rom 14:17—"For the kingdom of God is not food and drink but righteousness and peace and joy in the Holy Spirit."

19. 1 John 3:3—"And all who have this hope in him purify themselves, just as he is pure."

20. Heb 13:14—"For here we have no lasting city, but we are looking for the city that is to come." Eph 2:19—"So then you are no longer strangers and aliens, but you are citizens with the saints and also members of the household of God. . . ."

21. John 15:19—"If you belonged to the world, the world would love you as its own. Because you do not belong to the world, but I have chosen you out of the world—therefore the world hates you." John 17:14—"I have given them your word, and the world has hated them because they do not belong to the world, just as I do not belong to the world."

was in heaven.[22] The pursuit of holiness, the experience of love for Christ, and the exercises of worship and service in the fellowship of the saints, made the mortal life a true vestibule of eternity. When the people of God worshiped Him in unity and harmony out of a deep sense of adoration for His excellency and grace, from hearts abounding with love and joy, it was as if heaven came down within that worship. The blessings which we experienced in the previous life were both signs of and an actual entering into the more glorious benefits which we now enjoy fully in the final state.

Certain of our Savior's commands demonstrated the reality of a present participation in a future experience. We were commanded to lay up for ourselves treasures in heaven where they were beyond corruption and theft[23] and to seek those things which are above where Christ sits in exaltation and glory.[24] Both welcoming strangers into our fellowship and worship and crossing social and also economic boundaries which the surrounding society could not, showed the unconditional love of Christ in which we in eternity now bask.[25]

22. Eph 2:19—see note 20.

23. Matt 6:19–20—"Do not store up for yourselves treasures on earth, where moth and rust consume and where thieves break in and steal; but store up for yourselves treasures in heaven, where neither moth nor rust consumes and where thieves do not break in and steal."

24. Col 3:1–2—"So if you have been raised with Christ, seek the things that are above, where Christ is, seated at the right hand of God. Set your minds on things that are above, not on things that are on earth. . . ."

25. Luke 14:13–14—"But when you give a banquet, invite the poor, the crippled, the lame, and the blind. And you will be blessed, because they cannot repay you, for you will be repaid at the resurrection of the righteous." Matt 25:35–36—"[F]or I was hungry and you gave me food, I was thirsty and you gave me something to drink, I was a stranger and you welcomed me, I was naked and you gave me clothing, I was sick

In ways which we did not really understand at that time, the highest joy and pleasures of the former life were appetizers and pointers to the fuller and deeper joys and pleasures which we now enjoy in God's presence.[26] Our best desires were signposts to heaven. The healing miracles of Jesus pointed forward to His complete healing of all bodily ailments, including His conquering death by His very word; His miracles, such as calming the sea and turning the water to wine, were pictures of His display of omnipotence in redeeming of the entire created cosmos.

In a special sense the sacraments demonstrated, in a manner which transcended words, the realities of the world to come. Baptism pictured our union and identification with Christ in His finished atonement and His serving as our Great High Priest as well as the complete cleansing from all our sins. It also constituted a call for us to walk in newness of life.[27] The Lord's Supper was a taste of the Marriage Supper of the Lamb when Christ was present physically with us at that great feast in heaven when salvation in all of its fullness was experienced.[28] In it there was the

---

and you took care of me, I was in prison and you visited me." Matt 25:42–43—"[F]or I was hungry and you gave me no food, I was thirsty and you gave me nothing to drink, I was a stranger and you did not welcome me, naked and you did not give me clothing, sick and in prison and you did not visit me."

26. Ps 16:11—"You show me the path of life. In your presence there is fullness of joy; in your right hand are pleasures forevermore."

27. Rom 6:3–4—"Do you not know that all of us who have been baptized into Christ Jesus were baptized into his death? Therefore we have been buried with him by baptism into death, so that, just as Christ was raised from the dead by the glory of the Father, so we too might walk in newness of life."

28. Matt 26:29—"I tell you, I will never again drink of this fruit of the vine until that day when I drink it new with you in my Father's kingdom." Rev 19:7–9—"Let us rejoice and exult and give him the glory, for the marriage of the Lamb has come, and his bride has made herself ready; to her it has been granted to be clothed with fine linen, bright and

inauguration of the final state of the great Covenant of Grace in which salvation was brought to its eternally-intended consummation. As believers partook of the Table in the previous world and experienced the Eucharistic presence of Christ, something of the glorious future God has for His people broke through; it was as though they were transported from time to eternity and took their seats at the great Messianic banquet. The future invaded the present to fill that moment with the content of God's eternal purpose for His own. The fellowship of the Supper also was a part of the future fellowship we now enjoy above. It was as though when we partook of the Lord's Table in the mortal life that we were eating pieces of the wedding cake in advance. That future became an ineradicable part of the experience of the saints in their mortal lives, flavoring and conditioning their present experience.

---

pure—for the fine linen is the righteous deeds of the saints. And the angel said to me, 'Write this: Blessed are those who are invited to the marriage supper of the Lamb.' And he said to me, 'These are true words of God.'"

3

Seeing the Lord

Eternity

D<small>EAR</small> ,

As wonderful as those foretastes of heaven were, nothing could have prepared me adequately for the climax of my entire existence: seeing the Lord. Everything else pales in contrast to the privilege and wonder of seeing God. He is love itself, possessing love in its warmest degree, immeasurably and unimaginably kind, deep, and unsearchable in His innermost being. He exists in absolute purity, infinite goodness, with no needs which have to be met from outside Himself[1] or opposing principles (such as flesh and spirit, or darkness and light). He dwells in absolute holiness which far surpasses that relative holiness of the most unsoiled angels. He is the One whom Isaiah saw high and lifted up and worshiped by the seraphim.[2]

Though God is omnipresent (His being is present in its totality at all points of the created universe; the whole universe

---

1. Theologians of the former order sometimes said that God was "without passions" in that He has no needs outside Himself which have to be satisfied for His own happiness or well being. He cannot be manipulated or controlled. All His decisions are made totally out of His own sovereignty, freedom, omniscience, and independence.

2. Isa 6:1–5. After citing Isa 6:10, John writes, "Isaiah said this because he saw his glory and spoke about him" (John 12:41).

is as a single point on the graph to Him[3]), heaven is the fixed abode of His glorious manifestation.[4] It is God Himself who is always the centerpiece of the glory of heaven. Heaven in no way exhausts God's presence, but it is uniquely the place where His throne is located and the most nearly perfect worship and adoration occurs; it is rightly referred to as His dwelling place. It is in heaven that there is the demonstration and expression of God's infinite, eternal, and unchangeable divine glory. Furthermore, all the love experienced from human beings is but a drop compared to the inexhaustible love of God.

God, who exists outside of time and space, alone can satisfy the deepest longings of the human heart because He is the Creator of the world and of the persons who inhabit that world. Each human being is made both by Him and for Him; therefore, peace and rest are found only in Him. The enjoyment of God is the very essence of bliss. He is the soul's portion, forever satisfying the human heart. Heaven is the sheer, unlimited, and unhindered enjoyment of God. Death for the saint, which is very precious in the sight of God,[5] ushered me into the real experience of the goal of my existence: standing before the very glory of God.

The ultimate glory, the heaven of heavens, is seeing God Himself (sometimes called the beatific vision) not with the eyes of the body (because He is invisible and incorporeal), but the eyes of the soul. It is this great sight, this experience of intimacy with the divine, which provides the perfect fulfillment of all the

3. 2 Chr 2:6—"But who is able to build him a house, since heaven, even highest heaven, cannot contain him? Who am I to build a house for him, except as a place to make offerings before him?"

4. Ps 11:4—"The Lord is in his holy temple; the Lord's throne is in heaven."

5. Ps 116:15—"Precious in the sight of the Lord is the death of his faithful ones."

deepest human aspirations and desires. Freed from sin I experienced the highest possible privilege, the greatest ecstasy of glory, and the climax of salvation; I beheld God's glory unveiled in its fullness. No earthly enjoyment could ever begin to equal the unhindered view of God's glory, and I continue both to behold that glory of uncreated light and to make new discoveries of that Unsearchable Person. My supreme delight is in the full, unbroken, and intimate fellowship with the living God.

Seeing God was and is my greatest joy. In fact He is the heart and soul of heaven. What a thrill to be at home with Him and in His presence throughout all eternity. Being in His presence never grows old and stale, but is always fresh, vibrant, and stimulating. I cannot help but marvel that millions of people forfeited this eternity-long privilege, choosing in the previous world their own temporary pleasures and now-perished, momentary pursuits, rather than preparing for eternity. Enjoying the presence of God is truly the pearl of great price[6] to which no experience, object, or attainment in the previous world is worthy of being compared.[7]

This experience took place when I saw the Lamb of God on the throne of glory, sitting at the right hand of the majesty on high[8]; He is truly the paragon of all perfection, the very source and summit of all possible worth and excellence. The light of heaven is the radiant face of Jesus; the joy of heaven is His presence; and the theme is His worth. Heaven centers in Jesus Christ, resurrected, ascended, glorified, and crowned as absolute

---

6. Matt 13:45–46—"Again, the kingdom of heaven is like a merchant in search of fine pearls; on finding one pearl of great value, he went and sold all that he had and bought it."

7. Rom 8:18—"I consider that the sufferings of this present time are not worth comparing with the glory about to be revealed to us."

8. Heb 1:3—When he had made purification for sins, he sat down at the right hand of the Majesty on high. . . ."

ruler over all things. The universe bowed before this "King of Kings and Lord of Lords" when He conquered absolutely and forever death, the devil, disease, and all destruction. The physical creation was intended for Him—it revealed His wisdom and power. Likewise God's redemptive work was designed by God for Him[9]—it gave Him a bride, a family, an inheritance, and a community of worshipers who will sing "the Song of the Lamb" throughout all eternity:

> Great and amazing are your deeds, Lord God the Almighty! Just and true are your ways, King of the nations! Lord, who will not fear and glorify your name? For you alone are holy. All nations will come and worship before you, for your judgments have been revealed.[10]

Salvation demonstrates the brightest and most glorious radiance, beauty, and grace of Christ.

How glorious was the first ecstatic vision of the Savior in His celestial glory, who loved me and bought me with His own blood. Though I had believed in Him, loved Him, and served Him by faith, now I stood before His glorified physical presence. I will never forget the first opportunity of gazing on that Holy One, by whose righteousness and sacrifice alone I was there in heaven rather than suffering the agonies of Gehenna with billions of others, some of whom had actually committed fewer sins than I in the mortal life.[11] Looking into the eyes of

---

9. Col 1:16—"[F]or in him all things in heaven and on earth were created, things visible and invisible, whether thrones or dominions or rulers or powers—all things have been created through him and for him."

10. Rev 15:3–4.

11. Eph 1:7–8—"In Him we have redemption through His blood, the forgiveness of our trespasses, according to the riches of His grace, which

Him who is absolutely holy, infinitely loving, who as omniscient knows my every thought, word, and deed (he knows me intimately and exhaustively as no one else has ever known me), and then falling down to worship at His feet in adoration and thanksgiving, is an experience which cannot be captured either in earthly or heavenly languages. Peering into those eyes blazing with absolute holiness[12] and exuding ultimate and irresistible authority (He decrees the eternal destiny of every human being;[13]

He lavished upon us." Eph 2:8–9—For by grace you have been saved through faith, and this is not your own doing; it is the gift of God—not the result of works, so that no one may boast."

12. Rev 1:14—"His head and his hair were white as white wool, white as snow; his eyes were like a flame of fire . . . ."

13. Matt 25:34–46—"Then the king will say to those at his right hand, 'Come, you that are blessed by my Father, inherit the kingdom prepared for you from the foundation of the world; for I was hungry and you gave me food, I was thirsty and you gave me something to drink, I was a stranger and you welcomed me, I was naked and you gave me clothing, I was sick and you took care of me, I was in prison and you visited me.' Then the righteous will answer him, 'Lord, when was it that we saw you hungry and gave you food, or thirsty and gave you something to drink? And when was it that we saw you a stranger and welcomed you, or naked and gave you clothing? And when was it that we saw you sick or in prison and visited you?' And the king will answer them, 'Truly I tell you, just as you did it to one of the least of these who are members of my family, you did it to me.' Then he will say to those at his left hand, 'You that are accursed, depart from me into the eternal fire prepared for the devil and his angels; for I was hungry and you gave me no food, I was thirsty and you gave me nothing to drink, I was a stranger and you did not welcome me, naked and you did not give me clothing, sick and in prison and you did not visit me.' Then they also will answer, 'Lord, when was it that we saw you hungry or thirsty or a stranger or naked or sick or in prison, and did not take care of you?' Then he will answer them, 'Truly I tell you, just as you did not do it to one of the least of these, you did not do it to me.' And these will go away into eternal punishment, but the righteous into eternal life." John 5:22—"The Father judges no one but has given all judgment to the Son. . . ."

His word cannot be overruled[14]), is an experience which I cannot describe and can never forget. Here was the perfectly innocent Son of God who endured the awful wrath of God in my place[15] and had made intercession for me in heaven during my days of earthly struggle and toil[16] who now exercised absolute authority over all things. I knew that I was to blame for the scars on his hands, feet, and side.[17] Seeing His face was the ultimate realization of the intimacy and communion with God for which my soul had begun to long during the previous life.

I saw the majesty and glory of Christ reflected in His human nature and began to understand what Scripture means when

---

14. Matt 28:18—"And Jesus came and said to them, 'All authority in heaven and on earth has been given to me.'" John 3:36—"Whoever believes in the Son has eternal life; whoever disobeys the Son will not see life, but must endure God's wrath." Rev 3:7—"And to the angel of the church in Philadelphia write: 'These are the words of the holy one, the true one, who has the key of David, who opens and no one will shut, who shuts and no one opens. . . .'"

15. Isa 53:6—"All we like sheep have gone astray; we have all turned to our own way, and the Lord has laid on him the iniquity of us all." I Pet 2:24—"He himself bore our sins in his body on the cross, so that, free from sins, we might live for righteousness; by his wounds you have been healed."

16. Heb 7:25–27—"Consequently he is able for all time to save those who approach God through him, since he always lives to make intercession for them. For it was fitting that we should have such a high priest, holy, blameless, undefiled, separated from sinners, and exalted above the heavens. Unlike the other high priests, he has no need to offer sacrifices day after day, first for his own sins, and then for those of the people; this he did once for all when he offered himself."

17. Isa 53:4–5—"Surely he has borne our infirmities and carried our diseases; yet we accounted him stricken, struck down by God, and afflicted. But he was wounded for our transgressions, crushed for our iniquities; upon him was the punishment that made us whole, and by his bruises we are healed."

it says, "For in him the whole fullness of deity dwells bodily."[18] Through that body the moral attributes of God were expressed in an absolute way. While man was created in the relative image of God[19] (it was defaced at the Fall), Christ is the perfect and absolute image of God[20]; all that God is in His essential being is reflected in and through Him. He who had once suffered for my sins was now glorified in my same humanity[21] and occupies the throne at God's right hand, with all powers and authorities made subject to Him.[22] He reigns in triumphant majesty, sitting transcendently at God's right hand[23] with a radiance which far surpasses all created light, such as the earthly sun, and sparkles

---

18. Col 2:9.

19. Gen 1:27—"So God created humankind in his image, in the image of God he created them; male and female he created them." James 3:9—"With it we bless the Lord and Father, and with it we curse those who are made in the likeness of God. . . ."

20. Col 1:15—"He is the image of the invisible God, the firstborn of all creation." 2 Cor 4:4—"In their case the god of this world has blinded the minds of the unbelievers, to keep them from seeing the light of the gospel of the glory of Christ, who is the image of God."

21. 1 Cor 15:20—"But in fact Christ has been raised from the dead, the first fruits of those who have died." I John 3:2—"Beloved, we are God's children now; what we will be has not yet been revealed. What we do know is this: when he is revealed, we will be like him, for we will see him as he is."

22. Heb 2:8—"Thou madest him a little lower than the angels; thou crownedst him with glory and honour, and didst set him over the works of thy hands: Thou hast put all things in subjection under his feet. For in that he put all in subjection under him, he left nothing that is not put under him. But now we see not yet all things put under him" (KJV). Col 2:10—"[A]nd you have come to fullness in him, who is the head of every ruler and authority. . . ."

23. Heb 1:3—"When he had made purification for sins, he sat down at the right hand of the Majesty on high. . . ."

more spectacularly than all the diamonds in the previous world combined.[24] It was so glorious being welcomed into heaven by one in my same nature and one with whom I had long before been joined by faith.

Since the creation was brought into being through Christ's agency,[25] He is the Author of everything which is beautiful and perfect. The eyes of heaven center on Him. The saints behold Him with astonishment, adoration, gratitude, love, and wonder:

> They sing a new song: "You are worthy to take the scroll and to open its seals, for you were slaughtered and by your blood you ransomed for God saints from every tribe and language and people and nation; you have made them to be a kingdom and priests serving our God, and they will reign on earth." Then I looked, and I heard the voice of many angels surrounding the throne and the living creatures and the elders; they numbered myriads of myriads and thousands of thousands, singing with full voice, "Worthy is the Lamb that was slaughtered to receive power and wealth and wisdom and

---

24. Acts 26:13–15—Paul states, "[W]hen at midday along the road, your Excellency, I saw a light from heaven, brighter than the sun, shining around me and my companions. When we had all fallen to the ground, I heard a voice saying to me in the Hebrew language, 'Saul, Saul, why are you persecuting me? It hurts you to kick against the goads.' I asked, 'Who are you, Lord?' The Lord answered, 'I am Jesus whom you are persecuting.'" Heb 1:3—"He is the reflection of God's glory and the exact imprint of God's very being. . . ."

25. John 1:3—"All things were made by him; and without him was not any thing made that was made" (KJV). Col 1:16—"[F]or in him all things in heaven and on earth were created, things visible and invisible, whether thrones or dominions or rulers or powers—all things have been created through him and for him."

> might and honor and glory and blessing!" Then I heard every creature in heaven and on earth and under the earth and in the sea, and all that is in them, singing, "To the one seated on the throne and to the Lamb be blessing and honor and glory and might forever and ever!"[26]

What an indescribable experience it is also worshiping the Son of God with the innumerable hosts of those who were made to form His body as they were regenerated by the Holy Spirit. I continually worship him with human beings from every tribe, nation, and culture, all transformed and glorified, singing praise and adoration[27] with shouts louder than the greatest thunder on earth, roaring His adulation and worth (but never adequately).

We are now living in the answer to the amazing high priestly prayer of Jesus that His own be with Him and behold His eternal glory,[28] and are now embedded in a deeper experience of grace than was possible even in the most precious moments of spiritual blessing in the former world.[29] Our one ambition is to be near Him and to be like Him. The desire for heaven is the longing to be with Him, to be with this wonderful person more than it is to be in a particular place (heaven is where He

---

26. Rev 5:9–13.

27. Rev 7:9–10—"After this I looked, and there was a great multitude that no one could count, from every nation, from all tribes and peoples and languages, standing before the throne and before the Lamb, robed in white, with palm branches in their hands. They cried out in a loud voice, saying, 'Salvation belongs to our God who is seated on the throne, and to the Lamb!'"

28. John 17:24—"Father, I desire that those also, whom you have given me, may be with me where I am, to see my glory, which you have given me because you loved me before the foundation of the world."

29. Eph 2:7—"[S]o that in the ages to come he might show the immeasurable riches of his grace in kindness toward us in Christ Jesus."

is!). The experience of being joined with this Son of God, part of His bride,[30] is an exhilaration beyond the capabilities of any language to express. In heaven we behold God's glory in His face[31] and walk daily in the light of His presence. He appears all the more lovely to us as he reveals Himself more intimately and personally than was possible in the previous existence. What a delight to wear His name on our foreheads,[32] pointing to His ownership of us and our total obedience to Him. To be with Him is a joy which far eclipses any possible joy from the fallen creation. This Lamb is our Leader, our Guide, and our Head; He is our shield,[33] our sun, and our exceedingly great reward.[34]

30. Eph 5:25–27—"Husbands, love your wives, just as Christ loved the church and gave himself up for her, in order to make her holy by cleansing her with the washing of water by the word, so as to present the church to himself in splendor, without a spot or wrinkle or anything of the kind—yes, so that she may be holy and without blemish." Rev 21:2-3—"And I saw the holy city, the new Jerusalem, coming down out of heaven from God, prepared as a bride adorned for her husband. And I heard a loud voice from the throne saying, 'See, the home of God is among mortals. He will dwell with them as their God; they will be his peoples, and God himself will be with them. . . .'"

31. Rev 22:4—"[T]hey will see his face, and his name will be on their foreheads."

32. Rev 14:1—"Then I looked, and there was the Lamb, standing on Mount Zion! And with him were one hundred fortyfour thousand who had his name and his Father's name written on their foreheads." Rev 22:4—"[T]hey will see his face, and his name will be on their foreheads."

33. Ps 28:7—"The Lord is my strength and my shield." Psalm 84:11—"For the Lord God is a sun and shield; he bestows favor and honor."

34. Gen 15:1—"After these things the word of the Lord came to Abram in a vision, 'Do not be afraid, Abram, I am your shield; your reward shall be very great.'" Col 3:24—"[S]ince you know that from the Lord you will receive the inheritance as your reward; you serve the Lord Christ."

The ultimate benefit granted to any human being is truly the sight of God in the face of Jesus Christ.[35] In Him is the concentration of every virtue and excellence in perfection, the embodiment of grace, and the very fountain of all life.[36] He is the sovereign and absolute good, by whom all things are created and by whom all things are likewise preserved and governed.[37] He is also the giver of all goodness and happiness; in fact all goodness is derived from Him, including the goodness which we admire in virtuous people. All of God's benefits are channeled through Him to the created order.[38] He is the one Mediator between God and man[39] as well as between God and the created order.[40] He is everything; in fact, without Him the created order

---

35. Matt 5:8—"Blessed are the pure in heart, for they will see God." 2 Cor 4:6—"For it is the God who said, 'Let light shine out of darkness,' who has shone in our hearts to give the light of the knowledge of the glory of God in the face of Jesus Christ."

36. Col 2:3—"in whom [Christ] are hidden all the treasures of wisdom and knowledge." Col 2:9—"For in him the whole fulness of deity dwells bodily. . . ." John 5:26—"For just as the Father has life in himself, so he has granted the Son also to have life in himself. . . ." John 1:17—"The law indeed was given through Moses; grace and truth came through Jesus Christ."

37. Col 1:17—"He himself is before all things, and in him all things hold together." Heb 1:3—"He is the reflection of God's glory and the exact imprint of God's very being, and he sustains all things by his powerful word."

38. Col 1:19—"For in him all the fullness of God was pleased to dwell. . . ." 1 Cor 1: 30-31—"He is the source of your life in Christ Jesus, who became for us wisdom from God, and righteousness and sanctification and redemption, in order that, as it is written, 'Let the one who boasts, boast in the Lord.'"

39. 1 Tim 2:5—"For there is one God; there is also one mediator between God and humankind, Christ Jesus, himself human."

40. Col 1:20—"and through him God was pleased to reconcile to himself all things, whether on earth or in heaven, by making peace through

is nothing, but on the other hand, without the world, He is still everything.[41]

---

the blood of his cross." 1 Cor 15:28—"When all things are subjected to him, then the Son himself will also be subjected to the one who put all things in subjection under him, so that God may be all in all."

41. Col 1:17; Heb 13—see note 37.

4

The Judgment Seat of Christ

Eternity

DEAR _____,

The one experience of being with the glorified Christ, which was not totally pleasant, was standing before His judgment seat along with all other believers.[1] The discomfort came not from any defect in the Savior or the wonderful place which He had prepared for His people, but from my own failures as a regenerated person from the time of my conversion until I met Him in death.

It was a comfort to know that this Judge is the One who loves me (it was a judgment of love) and had given Himself as a sacrifice for me, that He harbors no ill will toward any of His own people, and that He knows the truth absolutely and exhaustively[2] and would declare only what is true. John states

---

1. 2 Cor 5:10—"For all of us must appear before the judgment seat of Christ, so that each may receive recompense for what has been done in the body, whether good or evil." Rom 14:10—"Why do you pass judgment on your brother or sister? Or you, why do you despise your brother or sister? For we will all stand before the judgment seat of God."

2. John 16:30—"Now we know that you know all things. . . ." John 18:4—"Then Jesus, knowing all that was to happen to him, came forward and asked them, 'Whom are you looking for?'. . . ."

that "from his mouth came a sharp, twoedged sword,"[3] which pictures the manner in which He speaks with both truth and authority. Without doubt the highest conceivable honor that any human being could ever receive was to hear directly from the Lord's mouth, "Well done, good and trustworthy slave; you have been trustworthy in a few things, I will put you in charge of many things; enter into the joy of your master."[4] All other commendations lapse into total insignificance compared to this praise. It has eternal implications, and the worth of the Giver makes this heavenly recognition most precious. Jesus had said, "Do not store up for yourselves treasures on earth, where moth and rust consume and where thieves break in and steal; but store up for yourselves treasures in heaven, where neither moth nor rust consumes and where thieves do not break in and steal."[5] Believers were promised "an inheritance that is imperishable, undefiled, and unfading, kept in heaven for you."[6]

As Scripture had declared, our works as believers followed us.[7] On the positive side not even an act as seemingly insignificant as the giving of a cup of cold water in our Lord's name was unremembered.[8] On the negative side men had to give an account for every evil committed, even for a single careless word which had been spoken.[9] It was a totally unique experience

3. Rev 1:16.

4. Matt 25:21.

5. Matt 6:19–20.

6. 2 Pet 1:4.

7. Rev 14:13—"And I heard a voice from heaven saying, 'Write this: Blessed are the dead who from now on die in the Lord.' 'Yes,' says the Spirit, 'they will rest from their labors, for their deeds follow them.'"

8. Matt 10:42—"[A]nd whoever gives even a cup of cold water to one of these little ones in the name of a disciple—truly I tell you, none of these will lose their reward."

9. Matt 12:36—"I tell you, on the day of judgment you will have to give an account for every careless word you utter."

standing before the omniscient Christ, before whose flaming eyes[10] everything is open and nothing is hidden,[11] who exists in absolute holiness, and who has total and absolute authority over all things (there is no appealing, reconsidering, or undoing what He decrees[12]). It was the single most sobering moment of my entire existence when I realized that He knew perfectly and remembered with absolute exactness every deed I had done, every word that I had spoken, and every thought that had gone through my mind. I had never before felt so absolutely exposed and laid open. Even when other human beings misunderstood my words or intentions, He knew them perfectly. On the other hand He could see the underlying selfishness, greed, and desire for self-glorification which had prompted many of my outwardly good acts and words. He saw through every excuse, evasion, or rationalization which I had ever put forth. He was ready to reveal what I really had been in the mortal life. I was thankful for every time where I had mortified my fleshly desires, but deeply sorrowful and ashamed for the times when I had followed the lusts of the flesh rather than the promptings of the indwelling Spirit as He enforced the admonitions and prohibitions of Holy Scripture. Even a momentary thought of lust, greed, or pride was totally abominable before His incomparable holiness.

The absolute seriousness of life was brought forcefully home to me as I observed fellow believers at the Judgment Seat

10. Rev 1:14—"[H]s eyes were like a flame of fire."

11. Heb 4:13—"And before him no creature is hidden, but all are naked and laid bare to the eyes of the one to whom we must render an account."

12. Matt 25:41—"Then he will say to those at his left hand, 'You that are accursed, depart from me into the eternal fire prepared for the devil and his angels.'" Matt 25:46—"And these will go away into eternal punishment, but the righteous into eternal life." Rev 1:18—"[A]nd I have the keys of Death and of Hades."

of Christ. Some were painfully confronted with the way they had wasted time, energy, and financial resources pursuing their selfish ends rather than investing themselves sacrificially in extending Christ's kingdom. Some were extremely sorrowful for the way they had not consistently mortified the flesh (David is an example[13]). Most saints regretted the feebleness of their love for Christ in the earthly life and wished that they had put forth more effort in His service, more time in studying His Word, and had developed deeper and more effective lives of prayer. Even those who had expended themselves totally for the Gospel, in a "bust a gut" fashion, considered their labors far too inadequate in the light of the Savior's great act of self-sacrifice for them. There were rewards graciously given to believers for their service in varying degrees according to the faithfulness of each saint. What really amazed me is how the Savior, in assessing rewards, did not forget even my smallest acts of charity; even acts of which I had hardly taken note, He remembered with pleasure because they glorified Him. I could not help but think of all the times in which I could have done an "extra" act of kindness (one above and beyond the call of duty) to someone and increased my Savior's joy, but shamefully I did not. If I had meditated on the reality and value of these eternal rewards (every earthly benefit pales into nothingness when contrasted with them), I would have been far more motivated to live selflessly and sacrificially in my earthly existence. I wished that I could have stood in the shoes of some of the saints at the judgment such as some of the martyrs who had suffered terrible agony for their testimony to Christ and certain missionaries who had expended themselves (health, resources, etc.) totally in getting the Gospel to those who had never heard of Christ.

---

13. 2 Sam 11.

At this judgment God, as always, was faithful to His promises. Those sins for which I had offered sincere confession and repentance, had been taken as far as the east is from the west;[14] God remembered them no more.[15] In His omniscience He of course knew cognitively that I had committed each one,[16] but He refused to allow any of these confessed sins to be reckoned judicially against me. These sins could not rise to accuse me or bring me shame and disgrace (the shame and disgrace had been suffered by the Savior on the cross). They were UB (under the blood); that is, they were completely forgiven because of His substitutionary death on my behalf. Therefore there was no condemnation upon me from the first instant that I believed in Jesus Christ.[17] But as my life was reviewed before Him like a huge video tape, where those now-forgiven sins had been committed, there were only blank spaces, as though nothing had occurred, when instead there could have been good works (fruit) which glorified my Lord and for which I was commended. When I saw the many blank spaces on the "tape," my eyes begin to water at the opportunities that I had squandered and for which I forfeited my Master's praise and His eternal rewards.[18]

In this sorrow I was reminded that my entire standing before God was based on His sovereign grace alone; I merited

---

14. Ps 103:12—"As far as the east is from the west, so far has He removes our transgressions from us."

15. Isa 43:25—"I, I am He who blots out your transgressions for my own sake, and I will not remember your sins."

16. Ps 139:4—"Even before is a word is on my tongue, O Lord, you know it completely." I John 3:20—"[F]or God is greater than our heart, and he knows everything."

17. Rom 8:1—"There is therefore now no condemnation for those who are in Christ Jesus."

18. 1 Cor 3:13–14—"I am He who blots out your transgressions for my own sake, and I will not remember your sins."

only His eternal disfavor in Gehenna. I remembered the words of Jesus, "So you also, when you have done all that you were ordered to do, say, 'We are worthless slaves; we have done only what we ought to have done!'"[19] In the end any reward that I received was of pure grace; God in His mercy remembered my faithful service done out of love for Him and obedience to His Word. Even my best works, mixed with many imperfections, were received as purified by the blood of Jesus.[20] God looked upon them as a parent looks on the woefully inadequate attempts of a child at pleasing him.

The fire of God thoroughly tested my life and its works with absolute comprehensiveness (nothing was excluded), consuming and removing the wood, hay, and straw, which were unworthy of a reward, and brought forth the precious stones which had glorified Christ and extended His kingdom.[21] It was bitter and painful seeing so much of what I had done being discarded, but oh what a thrill to see the Master's delight in that gold and silver which remained. The factors involved in the refining process were my stewardship of the resources which God had entrusted to me—including health, time, money, opportunities for ministry, and the use of the means of grace[22]—as well as my

---

19. Luke 17:10.

20. Heb 13:15—"I am He who blots out your transgressions for my own sake, and I will not remember your sins." 1 Pet 2:5—"[L]ike living stones, let yourselves be built into a spiritual house, to be a holy priesthood, to offer spiritual sacrifices acceptable to God through Jesus Christ."

21. 1 Cor 3:12–13—"Now if anyone builds on the foundation with gold, silver, precious stones, wood, hay, straw—the work of each builder will become visible, for the Day will disclose it, because it will be revealed with fire, and the fire will test what sort of work each has done."

22. The means of grace were those media through which the working of divine grace was engendered or strengthened in the heart during the

self-discipline, the faithful use of the spiritual gifts entrusted for me, the sacrifices I had made for the worldwide extension of the Gospel, the assistance given to those who were in need, and the faithfulness of my witness of His Gospel. I was held accountable for everything which the Master had put under my stewardship. In many instances I realized with great sadness and regret that I had buried a talent or wasted an opportunity instead of using it to bring manifold fruit for Him and His kingdom.[23] I regretted deeply how I had been so often preoccupied with earthly affairs to the exclusion of matters with eternal significance. How often my agenda had not been that which was really on the Savior's heart. The Judge reminded me how His Spirit had prompted me at one point to seek out a particular person and share the Gospel with him, but I had felt too busy and procrastinated, and then the person died suddenly, without anyone seriously confronting him with the claims of Christ. Indeed I was filled with shame at my disobedience, insensitivity to the Spirit, and spiritual dullness.

O the chagrin when I discovered that when I had hurt a fellow believer, that it was as though I had done the vicious act to Christ Himself—in fact He had suffered more than the fellow believer.[24] When I recalled some sins committed against fellow believers, I could hardly look into my Savior's eyes.

---

mortal life. They included primarily the written Word of God and the sacraments (baptism and the Lord's Supper), but secondarily encompassed Christian fellowship, prayer, and even providential chastening.

23. In the parable of the talents the one slave hears these words of condemnation: "Then you ought to have invested my money with the bankers, and on my return I would have received what was my own with interest" (Matt 25:14–30).

24. Isa 63:8–9—"[A]nd he became their savior in all their distress. It was no messenger or angel but his presence that saved them; in his love and in his pity he redeemed them; he lifted them up and carried them all

In a way which I had not expected I was also held responsible for the corporate sins of the larger groups with which I had been associated by geography, nationality, or family. As an American I shared the blame for the awful sin of abortion (the taking of the life of the innocent unborn),[25] the sin of homosexuality (to God it had been an utter abomination),[26] the sin of wastefulness and selfishness[27] in a world of great poverty and starvation, and the

---

the days of old." Matt 25:40—"And the king will answer them, 'Truly I tell you, just as you did it to one of the least of these who are members of my family, you did it to me.'" Acts 9:4–5—"He fell to the ground and heard a voice saying to him, 'Saul, Saul, why do you persecute me?' He asked, 'Who are you, Lord?' The reply came, 'I am Jesus, whom you are persecuting.'"

25. Exod 20:13—"You shall not murder." Ps 139:13–16—"For it was you who formed my inward parts; you knit me together in my mother's womb. I praise you, for I am fearfully and wonderfully made. Wonderful are your works; that I know very well. My frame was not hidden from you, when I was being made in secret, intricately woven in the depths of the earth. Your eyes beheld my unformed substance. In your book were written all the days that were formed for me, when none of them as yet existed."

26. Lev 18:22—"You shall not lie with a male as with a female; it is an abomination." Lev 20:13—"If a man lies with a male as with a woman, both of them have committed an abomination; they shall be put to death; their blood is upon them." Rom 1:27—"[A]nd in the same way also the men, giving up natural intercourse with women, were consumed with passion for one another. Men committed shameless acts with men and received in their own persons the due penalty for their error." 1 Cor 6:9–10—"Do you not know that wrongdoers will not inherit the kingdom of God? Do not be deceived! Fornicators, idolaters, adulterers, male prostitutes, sodomites, thieves, the greedy, drunkards, revilers, robbers—none of these will inherit the kingdom of God."

27. 1 Cor 10:24—"Do not seek your own advantage, but that of the other." Phil 2:4—"Let each of you look not to your own interests, but to the interests of others."

rejection of God's moral standards.[28] I also partook of the blame for the sins of my local community, my church, and my family. I wished I had followed Daniel's example of making corporate confession of sin even when I had not been the one committing the specific sin[29] and had voiced my opposition more strongly to the ungodliness around me.[30] I realize now how my silence had often implied consent to the unrighteous acts which had been committed in the vicinity where I lived.

Some believers who had been well known were highly rewarded for their faithfulness, diligence, and sacrifice in extending Christ's kingdom. They had always been abounding in the work of the Lord and their labors had not been in vain.[31] Though the judgment primarily concerned the deeds which were done in the mortal body,[32] it was amazing to see how there were rewards also for one's influence which extended beyond his or her own earthly existence though the lives of those affected, through one's testimony or reputation, through his writings such as books and

---

28. 1 Pet 1:15–16—"Instead, as he who called you is holy, be holy yourselves in all your conduct; for it is written, 'You shall be holy, for I am holy.'"

29. Daniel prayed, "Ah, Lord, great and awesome God, keeping covenant and steadfast love with those who love you and keep your commandments, we have sinned and done wrong, acted wickedly and rebelled, turning aside from your commandments and ordinances" (Dan 9:3–19).

30. Eph 5:11–12—"Take no part in the unfruitful works of darkness, but instead expose them. For it is shameful even to mention what such people do secretly. . . ."

31. 1 Cor 15:58—"Therefore, my beloved, be steadfast, immovable, always excelling in the work of the Lord, because you know that in the Lord your labor is not in vain."

32. 2 Cor 5:10—"For all of us must appear before the judgment seat of Christ, so that each may receive recompense for what has been done in the body, whether good or evil."

articles, through sermons, and even through institutions and churches which had been planted and established.

However, it was very sobering seeing some who had achieved great notoriety in the Christian world, having everything consumed and escaping with no rewards except their eternal salvation. God saw through their self-concern and kingdom-building attitude. They emerged with the smell of smoke on them.[33] How dreadful it was beholding their whole lives being declared useless and being consumed. On the other hand, it was astounding seeing some real "dark horses," those who had been unrecognized and virtually unknown in the Christian world at large (or were misunderstood and unappreciated by the Christian world), but who received huge rewards for their self-denial, diligence, faithfulness in prayer, their deeds of the most humble service, their development of personal virtues such as holiness and humility, and their personal witness for Christ.[34] God saw many who had invested what seemed to be very small and almost insignificant

---

33. 1 Cor 3:10–15.

34. Luke 6:35—"But love your enemies, do good, and lend, expecting nothing in return. Your reward will be great, and you will be children of the Most High; for he is kind to the ungrateful and the wicked." Matt 25:34–40—"Then the king will say to those at his right hand, 'Come, you that are blessed by my Father, inherit the kingdom prepared for you from the foundation of the world; for I was hungry and you gave me food, I was thirsty and you gave me something to drink, I was a stranger and you welcomed me, I was naked and you gave me clothing, I was sick and you took care of me, I was in prison and you visited me.' Then the righteous will answer him, 'Lord, when was it that we saw you hungry and gave you food, or thirsty and gave you something to drink? And when was it that we saw you a stranger and welcomed you, or naked and gave you clothing? And when was it that we saw you sick or in prison and visited you?' And the king will answer them, 'Truly I tell you, just as you did it to one of the least of these who are members of my family, you did it to me.'"

items, but had given "the widow's mite,"[35] which represented all that they had, and they joyfully invested it in His service; their rewards were enormous.

After the regular judgment there was a special session for teachers in which much stricter standards of evaluation were imposed.[36] Included in the "teachers" were all those who had opportunity for significant influence on others such as pastors, academic professors, writers, counselors, and others in leadership roles. They were held accountable both for their own lives and also for the results in the lives of those they mentored or influenced. Some of these saints received the highest possible commendation and rewards that were astronomical because they had followed Paul's command, "[W]hat you have heard from me through many witnesses entrust to faithful people who will be able to teach others as well."[37] They had discipled men who became disciplers of others in full obedience to the Great Commission given by Christ to His church.[38] The evangelists who had turned many to righteousness were highly praised.[39] On the other hand, to many the Master said sharply as God said

---

35. Luke 21:2–3—"[H]e also saw a poor widow put in two small copper coins. He said, 'Truly I tell you, this poor widow has put in more than all of them. . . .'" Also Mark 12:41–44.

36. Jas 3:1—"Not many of you should become teachers, my brothers and sisters, for you know that we who teach will be judged with greater strictness."

37. 2 Tim 2:2.

38. Matt 28:19–20—"Go therefore and make disciples of all nations, baptizing them in the name of the Father and of the Son and of the Holy Spirit, and teaching them to obey everything that I have commanded you. And remember, I am with you always, to the end of the age.'"

39. Dan 12:3—"Those who are wise shall shine like the brightness of the sky, and those who lead many to righteousness, like the stars forever and ever."

to Eliphaz and his two friends, "My wrath is kindled against you and against your two friends; for you have not spoken of me what is right, as my servant Job has."[40] These individuals had not carefully taught what God had revealed in Holy Scripture, but had put forth their own subjective ideas and idiosyncracies, catering to those with "itching ears."[41] They had acted more like hirelings[42] than as Christ's undershepherds of the flock entrusted to them[43]; instead of the glory of God and the spiritual health of the flock, they had pursued only their own welfare. The look of dismay on their faces at the judgment was indescribable.

Believers who refused to listen to the Word of God experienced the strong disfavor of the Judge. He reminded them of the times His faithful servants had studied the Word faithfully and proclaimed it truthfully before them, but they refused to listen and to obey.[44] In the same way those who had refused

---

40. Job 42:7.

41. 2 Tim 4:3—"For the time is coming when people will not put up with sound doctrine, but having itching ears, they will accumulate for themselves teachers to suit their own desires. . . ."

42. John 10:12–13—"The hired hand, who is not the shepherd and does not own the sheep, sees the wolf coming and leaves the sheep and runs away—and the wolf snatches them and scatters them. The hired hand runs away because a hired hand does not care for the sheep."

43. Acts 20:28—"Keep watch over yourselves and over all the flock, of which the Holy Spirit has made you overseers, to shepherd the church of God that he obtained with the blood of his own Son." 1 Pet 5:1–2—"Now as an elder myself and a witness of the sufferings of Christ, as well as one who shares in the glory to be revealed, I exhort the elders among you to tend the flock of God that is in your charge, exercising the oversight, not under compulsion but willingly, as God would have you do it—not for sordid gain but eagerly."

44. Jas 1:22—"But be doers of the word, and not merely hearers who deceive themselves." Hebrews 5:11—"About this we have much to say that is hard to explain, since you have become dull in understanding."

godly, biblical counsel attempted by Christ's faithful servants, were reprimanded for their hardness of heart.[45]

Though in a real sense God Himself is the supreme reward,[46] He rewarded His faithful people with incorruptible crowns.[47] It was thrilling beholding believers, some of whom I had known and with whom I had enjoyed precious fellowship, receiving the crown of life given to those who had persevered under trial[48]; in fact, being with Christ and enjoying eternal life is the crown of life. Christ's diligent disciples also received the crown of rejoicing,[49] the crown of glory,[50] and the crown of righteousness.[51] Those who received these rewards had obeyed the inspired instruction, "[H]old fast what you have, in order that no one take your crown."[52] Each faithful believer also received rewards which were unique and particular to his labor and the

---

45. Heb 4:7—"Today, if you hear His voice, do not harden your hearts."

46. Lam 3:24—"'The Lord is my portion,' says my soul, 'therefore I will hope in him.'" Ps 16:5—"The Lord is my chosen portion and my cup; you hold my lot."

47. 1 Cor 9:25—"Athletes exercise self-control in all things; they do it to receive a perishable wreath, but we an imperishable one."

48. Jas 1:12—"Blessed is anyone who endures temptation. Such a one has stood the test and will receive the crown of life that the Lord has promised to those who love him." Rev 2:10—"Be faithful until death, and I will give you the crown of life."

49. 1 Thess 2:19—"For what is our hope or joy or crown of boasting before our Lord Jesus at his coming? Is it not you?"

50. 1 Pet 5:4—"And when the chief shepherd appears, you will receive the crown of glory that never fades away."

51. 2 Tim 4:8—"From now on there is reserved for me the crown of righteousness, which the Lord, the righteous judge, will give me on that day, and not only to me but also to all who have longed for his appearing."

52. Rev 3:11.

distinct contribution which he had made to building God's kingdom.[53] As God demonstrated endless beauty and variety in the created order, so he showed awesome creativity and variety in the distribution of rewards that left me absolutely breathless. It was spellbinding seeing how the rewards were so exquisitely tailored to the unique personality and contribution made by each faithful disciple. These rewarded saints absolutely basked in God's approval and commendation, but they viewed what was granted as constituting a suitable (though hopelessly inadequate in their eyes) offering of thanksgiving and praise to be laid at the feet of the Lamb of God who alone is worthy to be praised.[54] Those who escaped from the fire unrewarded looked so embarrassed and forlorn as their more faithful comrades joyfully laid their rewards at the feet of the Savior.[55] How tragic it was for them to have nothing tangible by which to offer gratitude and praise to the One who had given Himself for them.

Christ granted His faithful disciples the privilege of reigning with Him in the new heavens and the new earth. He gave us the authority to rule over the nations and to act as His viceregents in the government of the new order.[56] It was amazing

53. 1 Cor 3:8—"The one who plants and the one who waters have a common purpose, and each will receive wages according to the labor of each."

54. Rev 5:12—"Worthy is the Lamb that was slaughtered to receive power and wealth and wisdom and might and honor and glory and blessing!"

55. Rev 4:10—"[T]he twentyfour elders fall before the one who is seated on the throne and worship the one who lives forever and ever; they cast their crowns before the throne, singing. . . ."

56. Rev 2:26–28—"To everyone who conquers and continues to do my works to the end, I will give authority over the nations; to rule them with an iron rod, as when clay pots are shattered—even as I also received authority from my Father. To the one who conquers I will also give the morning star." Rev 3:21—"To the one who conquers I will give a place

watching believers I had known now sharing Christ's throne. However, the specific areas of authority and responsibility entrusted to each glorified believer were determined by the degree of his (or her) faithfulness, stewardship, and overall commitment to Christ during his (or her) earthly life. The issue was not the size of the ministry in the previous order, but the quality of stewardship which was offered to the omniscient Master.[57] Faithfulness in a few matters dictated the capacity or responsibility with which one was entrusted in the larger matters of the eternal kingdom.

After this great evaluation of God's people I heard thousands gasping with words like, "All this for my tiny efforts." Nothing had fallen between the cracks in the omniscient Judge's appraisal of His servants. On the other hand, many saints were heard exclaiming, "If I had only known how the Savior would reward His own exactly, my life would have been so different." The fact that our whole lives were reviewed by the Judge and every part entailed the opportunity for rewards, brought home so forcefully before me the importance of the mortal life and how carefully it ought to have been invested in the light of eternity.

---

with me on my throne, just as I myself conquered and sat down with my Father on his throne."

57. Matt 25:20–23—"Then the one who had received the five talents came forward, bringing five more talents, saying, 'Master, you handed over to me five talents; see, I have made five more talents.' His master said to him, 'Well done, good and trustworthy slave; you have been trustworthy in a few things, I will put you in charge of many things; enter into the joy of your master.' And the one with the two talents also came forward, saying, 'Master, you handed over to me two talents; see, I have made two more talents.' His master said to him, 'Well done, good and trustworthy slave; you have been trustworthy in a few things, I will put you in charge of many things; enter into the joy of your master.'" Luke 19:17—"He said to him, 'Well done, good slave! Because you have been trustworthy in a very small thing, take charge of ten cities.'"

5

The Promises of God Fulfilled

Eternity

D^{EAR} _____,

It was an absolutely awesome sight, after that great day of judgment, seeing the former heavens being burned up and passing away with a huge roar, the elements being destroyed with intense heat, and the earth with its works being consumed.[1] I realized that the idols of millions of people (whether it was material objects, human recognition, positions of power and influence, personal accomplishments, or sensual pleasure) were part of that huge conflagration; that what they had lived and died for, sometimes even stealing and murdering to attain, was no more. Indeed the world and all its lusts had passed away and would never be known again. However, those who had done the

---

1. 1 Pet 3:10–13—"But the day of the Lord will come like a thief, and then the heavens will pass away with a loud noise, and the elements will be dissolved with fire, and the earth and everything that is done on it will be disclosed. Since all these things are to be dissolved in this way, what sort of persons ought you to be in leading lives of holiness and godliness, waiting for and hastening the coming of the day of God, because of which the heavens will be set ablaze and dissolved, and the elements will melt with fire?"

will of God had an eternal abode and were about to inherit the eternal promises of God.[2]

During the mortal life I had studied the prophetic passages of the Bible and believed them thoroughly. While some writers and speakers had published, in an authoritative manner, charts and diagrams which they claimed showed how all the particular events of prophecy would fit together, the more I studied the more I struggled to find a harmonization which would do justice to all the biblical texts and assertions. The data seemed to defy systematization. In fact, none of the great systems of eschatology seemed to do justice to all the Biblical data; each one either omitted or manipulated some parts or texts to make them fit its own particular system. But in God's perfect timing and according to His infinite wisdom, I was actually able to see all the details of prophecy being fulfilled. Everything that God had declared came to pass exactly as He had promised in Holy Scripture. I was reminded that "the words of the Lord are pure words: as silver tried in a furnace of earth, purified seven times."[3] Even the smallest details of God's promises had come to pass.[4] As Joshua declared to the Israelites, "[Y]ou know in your hearts and in all your souls that no one word of all the good words which the Lord your God spoke concerning you has failed; all have been fulfilled for you, not one of them has failed,"[5] so I can testify that not a single word spoken by God has failed. In partic-

---

2. 1 John 2:16–17—"[F]or all that is in the world—the desire of the flesh, the desire of the eyes, the pride in riches—comes not from the Father but from the world. And the world and its desire are passing away, but those who do the will of God live forever."

3. Ps 12:6 (KJV).

4. Matt 5:18—"For truly I tell you, until heaven and earth pass away, not one letter, not one stroke of a letter, will pass from the law until all is accomplished."

5. Josh 23:14.

ular the purposes of God, drawn in eternity before the previous creation was granted its existence, were all brought to full and perfect completion; not the smallest iota remained unfulfilled.[6] How awesome was His sovereignty and wisdom in orchestrating all the ends and means, with billions of seeming contingencies and human agencies, so that His designs came about exactly as He had intended. It was truly awe-inspiring witnessing the total vindication of His holiness and justice in the defeat and judgment of evil and wicked men and angels.[7] Not a single sin was left unpunished.[8] His great purpose in bringing all of creation into subjection to His eternal Son was certainly fulfilled.[9] How glorious watching every knee bow and every tongue confess that Jesus Christ is Lord.[10] One group bowed in shame and disgrace

---

6. Eph 1:8–11—"With all wisdom and insight he has made known to us the mystery of his will, according to his good pleasure that he set forth in Christ, as a plan for the fullness of time, to gather up all things in him, things in heaven and things on earth. In Christ we have also obtained an inheritance, having been destined according to the purpose of him who accomplishes all things according to his counsel and will. . . ." Eph 3:11—"This was in accordance with the eternal purpose that he has carried out in Christ Jesus our Lord. . . ."

7. 1 Cor 15:24–25—"Then comes the end, when he hands over the kingdom to God the Father, after he has destroyed every ruler and every authority and power. For he must reign until he has put all his enemies under his feet."

8. Ezek 18:20—"The person who sins shall die." Rom 6:23—"For the wages of sin is death. . . ."

9. Eph 1:9–10—see Note 6. Eph 1:20–22—"God put this power to work in Christ when he raised him from the dead and seated him at his right hand in the heavenly places, far above all rule and authority and power and dominion, and above every name that is named, not only in this age but also in the age to come. And he has put all things under his feet and has made him the head over all things for the church. . . ."

10. Phil 2:9–11—"Therefore God also highly exalted him and gave him the name that is above every name, so that at the name of Jesus every

before the One they had rejected and despised; the other bowed in love, adoration, and thanksgiving before the One in whom they had believed and whose yoke they had gladly accepted. I thought that heaven was going to explode with joy as history closed on that great crescendo. The final word spoken over human history was "Jesus Christ is Lord."

I can never forget the experience of seeing the new heaven and the new earth for the first time.[11] What I had studied, with its deep symbolism, employing images drawn from the older earth, accommodated to my feeble, limited, and what I now realize was naive understanding, in Revelation 21 and 22, though beautiful in its description of this new world, was now before my very own eyes, causing them to feast with rapturous delight. Heaven was indeed beyond the boundaries of the mortal imagination and the capabilities of all earthly languages to convey. There was nothing in the previous order which could adequately represent or illustrate this marvelous new world. No writer, artist, or philosopher from the old order had even gotten close to picturing this city as it really is. The best which the former world had to offer was such a dim, even childish, reflection of the final creation. It was obvious that the Creator had saved the best wine until the last. Before me stood a place of indescribable splendor, far transcending anything I had ever previously seen, experienced, or even imagined. The city was fresh, stimulat-

---

knee should bend, in heaven and on earth and under the earth, and every tongue should confess that Jesus Christ is Lord, to the glory of God the Father."

11. Isa 65:17—"For I am about to create new heavens and a new earth. . . ." Isa 66:22—"For as the new heavens and the new earth, which I will make, shall remain before me. . . ." 2 Pet 3:13—"But, in accordance with his promise, we wait for new heavens and a new earth, where righteousness is at home."

ing, vibrant, with an eternal newness about it, which produced within me a constant and ever-deepening sense of wonder.

Noah and his family had experienced what it was to return to a cleansed, renewed earth after the comprehensive removal of the wicked by God's decisive judgment.[12] But this was a whole new universe, and one totally and forever purged of everything which had been evil and opposed God and His holy purposes.[13] There had been a cosmic remodeling which was of such a stupendous and momentous character that only the original Creator could bring it about. That same omniscience, omnipotence, and absolute authority which had originally brought the creation into being out of previously non-existing materials,[14] had operated once more, but this time in a far more glorious and final (i.e., irreversible) way. The creation had been renovated so that now all things were made new.[15] How amazing to see the instantaneous and total obedience of the entire physical universe to the expressed word of the Almighty. The old had been dissolved and recast into purity, beauty, and glory which will, throughout all the endless ages of eternity, never be soiled and contaminated by sin. At last the curse put justly upon the earth

12. Gen 8.

13. Rev 21:27—"But nothing unclean will enter it, nor anyone who practices abomination or falsehood, but only those who are written in the Lamb's book of life." Rev 22:15—"Outside are the dogs and sorcerers and fornicators and murderers and idolaters, and everyone who loves and practices falsehood."

14. Gen 1:1—"In the beginning when God created the heavens and the earth. . . ." Rom 4:17—"[I]n the presence of the God in whom he believed, who gives life to the dead and calls into existence the things that do not exist." Heb 11:3—"By faith we understand that the worlds were prepared by the word of God, so that what is seen was made from things that are not visible."

15. Isa 65:17—see note 11. Rev 21:5—"And the one who was seated on the throne said, 'See, I am making all things new.'"

by the Creator after man's sin, bringing disease, pain, and death with all their accompanying sorrows and agony, was lifted, never to be imposed again.[16]

What the resurrected body is to the former mortal body, the new creation is to the old creation. It is amazing living in a physical world without disasters like earthquakes, tornadoes, famines, and floods and a human world without doctors, dentists, hospitals, and cemeteries. It seemed strange at first to be living in a world without police, without jails, without armies, without locks, and without security systems. It is so different living in a world where no one harbors ill will against you, no one covets what you have, no one slanders you, and everyone always tells the truth. It is also a world where there are no labels such as "classified" and "top secret," since everything is open and transparent. The only "secrets" are the mysteries involved in God's inner depths, which He allows us, very slowly and gradually because of our creaturely limitations, to penetrate though we realize that throughout all the endless ages it will be a study which we will never be able to complete; the curriculum far outdistances our greatest possible capacity. It is indeed a school with no graduation.[17]

What we had experienced as personal regeneration was now seen in the larger cosmic dimension as the universe itself was reborn. The renewal was eternal and complete; the earth indeed rose from its former groanings to a new and previously

---

16. Rev 22:3—"And there shall be no more curse . . ." (KJV).

17. Rom 11:33–34—"O the depth of the riches and wisdom and knowledge of God! How unsearchable are his judgments and how inscrutable his ways! 'For who has known the mind of the Lord? Or who has been his counselor?'" Eph 2:7—"so that in the ages to come he might show the immeasurable riches of his grace in kindness toward us in Christ Jesus."

unimaginable glory.[18] What Satan ruined has now been made into a home for the redeemed which is better by far. The end surpasses the beginning in every detail. The new abode is the magnificent palace where the redeemed dwell with their Maker and Redeemer. Not the slightest detail of the new order is inferior to the former world. The whole of the new creation displays a unity and a harmony as all things have been brought into reconciliation with God through Christ.[19]

It was in this state of consummated salvation that we were granted the ability to fulfill our original purpose and mandate as human beings—to exercise dominion as God's vice-regents over the earth.[20] Since human beings are no longer weighed down with sin and depravity, the activity of those now completely filled with the Holy Spirit, living in perfect obedience to God,

18. Rom 8:21–22—"that the creation itself will be set free from its bondage to decay and will obtain the freedom of the glory of the children of God. We know that the whole creation has been groaning in labor pains until now. . . ." Acts 3:21—"who must remain in heaven until the time of universal restoration that God announced long ago through his holy prophets." Rev 21:2—"And I saw the holy city, the new Jerusalem, coming down out of heaven from God, prepared as a bride adorned for her husband."

19. Col 1:20—"[A]nd through him God was pleased to reconcile to himself all things, whether on earth or in heaven, by making peace through the blood of his cross."

20. Gen 1:28—"God blessed them, and God said to them, 'Be fruitful and multiply, and fill the earth and subdue it; and have dominion over the fish of the sea and over the birds of the air and over every living thing that moves upon the earth.'" Ps 8:4–8—"[W]hat are human beings that you are mindful of them, mortals that you care for them? Yet you have made them a little lower than God, and crowned them with glory and honor. You have given them dominion over the works of your hands; you have put all things under their feet, all sheep and oxen, and also the beasts of the field, the birds of the air, and the fish of the sea, whatever passes along the paths of the seas."

blends together to form a glorious and resplendent culture. It is astounding to see the image of God reflected so perfectly in the gigantic orchestra of redeemed humanity, with each individual reflecting that image in a unique way and the combined images all blending into a harmonious and magnificent reflection of the Creator.

How glorious it was as all heaven rejoiced at the much anticipated final union of Christ and His chosen bride made up of all the redeemed from all ages.[21] As the morning stars sang together and all the sons of God shouted for joy when the original earth was created,[22] what a song of glory and adoration was sung by both the angelic hosts and the great throng of redeemed humanity as God brought before billions of awestruck eyes the new, eternal created order. God's eternal purpose was brought to completion in the final restitution of the physical universe. His eternal wisdom was most greatly displayed in the consummated salvation of those once depraved men and women who were purified through the atoning work of God's Son and now stand remade in the very image of Christ.[23] What an amazing contrast between what these deserved because of both the sin of the race

---

21. Rev 21:9–10—"'Come, I will show you the bride, the wife of the Lamb.' And in the spirit he carried me away to a great, high mountain and showed me the holy city Jerusalem coming down out of heaven from God." Rev 5:9—"You are worthy to take the scroll and to open its seals, for you were slaughtered and by your blood you ransomed for God saints from every tribe and language and people and nation. . . ."

22. Job 38:7.

23. Eph 3:9–11—"[A]nd to make everyone see what is the plan of the mystery hidden for ages in God who created all things; so that through the church the wisdom of God in its rich variety might now be made known to the rulers and authorities in the heavenly places. This was in accordance with the eternal purpose that he has carried out in Christ Jesus our Lord." 1 Pet 2:9—"But you are a chosen race, a royal priesthood, a holy nation, God's own people, in order that you may proclaim the mighty acts of him who called you out of darkness into his marvelous light."

and their own personal sins and the quality of grace which they have received, grace which shows forth the wisdom and love of God in ways which makes the angels gasp.[24] How marvelous to be part of that huge prism that reflects so brightly the beauty of the uncreated light which emanates from the Creator Himself.[25]

Although the fact was substantially demonstrated by Christ's resurrection appearances and His bodily ascension, we now know by our own experience that heaven is a real place, one which is tangible and physical, not just some state of mind or imagined reality. It is a place where people in real bodies live, interact, and serve their Creator though it can be viewed only through the eyes of the glorified body. The lost have never been allowed even to see this new world though they know intuitively now that they sacrificed eternal blessedness for their momentary and perverted pleasures in the former world and thereby reaped eternal misery.[26]

---

24. 1 Pet 1:12—"It was revealed to them that they were serving not themselves but you, in regard to the things that have now been announced to you through those who brought you good news by the Holy Spirit sent from heaven—things into which angels long to look!"

25. 1 John 1:5-7—"God is light and in him there is no darkness at all. If we say that we have fellowship with him while we are walking in darkness, we lie and do not do what is true; but if we walk in the light as he himself is in the light, we have fellowship with one another, and the blood of Jesus his Son cleanses us from all sin."

26. Heb 11:25—"choosing rather to share illtreatment with the people of God than to enjoy the fleeting pleasures of sin." Heb 12:16—"that there be no immoral or godless person like Esau, who sold his own birthright for a single meal." 1 John 2:16–17—"[F]or all that is in the world—the desire of the flesh, the desire of the eyes, the pride in riches—comes not from the Father but from the world. And the world and its desire are passing away, but those who do the will of God live forever." Rev 14:11—"And the smoke of their torment goes up forever and ever. There is no rest day or night for those who worship the beast and its image and

Certainly God's invisible attributes, especially His wisdom and power, were revealed though the created order of the former world,[27] but the new creation mirrors His transcendent greatness much more exquisitely and in a way which is beyond all standards of comparison. His glory illuminates the entire new universe, making the old sun seem like only a small candle.[28] The works of His hands furnish our glorified minds with matters which are inexhaustible and profound, producing continuing gasps of wonder, awe, and spontaneous worship. The blessedness, glory, and perfection of the Creator are thundered constantly from the excellence of His handiwork and His providential rule over the new heavens and the new earth.

The presence of God Himself fills the entire city and every glorified soul so that no temple is needed; God Himself is the temple.[29] We have immediate access into His presence and worship Him directly.[30] It was really startling watching the distinction between heaven and earth being removed forever and heaven and

---

for anyone who receives the mark of its name."

27. Rom 1:20—"Ever since the creation of the world his eternal power and divine nature, invisible though they are, have been understood and seen through the things he has made. So they are without excuse. . . ."

28. Isa 24:23—"Then the moon will be abashed, and the sun ashamed; for the Lord of hosts will reign on Mount Zion and in Jerusalem, and before his elders he will manifest his glory." Isa 60:19—"The sun shall no longer be your light by day, nor for brightness shall the moon give light to you by night; but the Lord will be your everlasting light, and your God will be your glory." Rev 22:5—"And there will be no more night; they need no light of lamp or sun, for the Lord God will be their light, and they will reign forever and ever."

29. Rev 21:22—"I saw no temple in the city, for its temple is the Lord God the Almighty and the Lamb."

30. Rev 22:4—"they will see his face, and his name will be on their foreheads."

earth finally becoming one.[31] Men now are granted the inestimable privilege of sharing God's dwelling place for ever.

The New Jerusalem, described symbolically by John the apostle as being twelve thousand stadia (or between 1,400 and 1,500 miles) square[32] certainly dwarfs any city of the former world. Its immensity points to the grand and lavish life in heaven and the fact that there is room for all who responded to the invitation of the Gospel, which was indeed a huge number beyond what we could have conceptualized during our mortal lives. As the abode of the Almighty it is a most holy city, and only those who have been made holy by the blood of the Lamb have access to it. In the place of our previously polluted environment, now we experience the radiant, gleaming glory of God Himself. This city is truly the fitting abode for those who have been made perfect by divine grace. All negatives have been replaced by positives, and every "if only" has been replaced by gratitude and thanksgiving for that which is and will always be.[33]

This city sparkles like a diamond, reflecting God's very nature with astonishing beauty, as symbolized by John's employment of the precious jewels which constituted the most glorious

---

31. Rev 21:3—"And I heard a loud voice from the throne saying, 'See, the home of God is among mortals. He will dwell with them as their God; they will be his peoples, and God himself will be with them. . . .'"

32. Rev 21:16.

33. Rev 21:4—"[H]e will wipe every tear from their eyes. Death will be no more; mourning and crying and pain will be no more, for the first things have passed away." Rev 21:6—"Then he said to me, 'It is done! I am the Alpha and the Omega, the beginning and the end. To the thirsty I will give water as a gift from the spring of the water of life.'" Rev 22:1–2—"Then the angel showed me the river of the water of life, bright as crystal, flowing from the throne of God and of the Lamb through the middle of the street of the city. On either side of the river is the tree of life with its twelve kinds of fruit, producing its fruit each month; and the leaves of the tree are for the healing of the nations."

images of his day.[34] Indeed the whole city shines more brightly than any star of the previous universe. It radiates with an eternal brilliance from God, the source of all light, which would have left the sun of the former world in embarrassment.[35]

At the center of the city is the throne of God, which represents both His absolute sovereignty and His total worthiness in both character and divinity to be worshiped. Because it is the place where God dwells, it is a place exuding great glory,[36] glory so great that all the sufferings of the mortal life are rendered as nothing in comparison.[37] It is also a place of magnificent beauty,[38]

---

34. Rev 21:18–21—"The wall is built of jasper, while the city is pure gold, clear as glass. The foundations of the wall of the city are adorned with every jewel; the first was jasper, the second sapphire, the third agate, the fourth emerald, the fifth onyx, the sixth carnelian, the seventh chrysolite, the eighth beryl, the ninth topaz, the tenth chrysoprase, the eleventh jacinth, the twelfth amethyst. And the twelve gates are twelve pearls, each of the gates is a single pearl, and the street of the city is pure gold, transparent as glass."

35. Isa 24:23—see note 28.

36. Ps 29:9—"[A]nd in his temple all say 'Glory!'"

37. Rom 8:18—"I consider that the sufferings of this present time are not worth comparing with the glory about to be revealed to us."

38. Ps 50:2—"Out of Zion, the perfection of beauty, God shines forth." Isa 33:17—"Your eyes will see the king in his beauty. . . ."

of immortality and incorruptibility,[39] of love,[40] and of fullness of joy.[41] Its great wall[42] symbolizes its inviolable security and its total separation from everything that is polluted and unclean. It also reminds the glorified inhabitants that they were once on the other side of the wall without access into God's presence, totally devoid of the absolute holiness which He requires for entrance.[43]

39. Rev 20:6—"Blessed and holy are those who share in the first resurrection. Over these the second death has no power. . . ." Rev 21:4—see note 33. 1 Cor 15:42—"So it is with the resurrection of the dead. What is sown is perishable, what is raised is imperishable. . . ." 1 Cor 15:53–55—"For this perishable body must put on imperishability, and this mortal body must put on immortality. When this perishable body puts on imperishability, and this mortal body puts on immortality, then the saying that is written will be fulfilled: 'Death has been swallowed up in victory.' 'Where, O death, is your victory? Where, O death, is your sting?'"

40. John 17:23—"I in them and you in me, that they may become completely one, so that the world may know that you have sent me and have loved them even as you have loved me."

41. Ps 16:11—"You show me the path of life. In your presence there is fullness of joy; in your right hand are pleasures forevermore." Isa 65:17–19—"For I am about to create new heavens and a new earth; the former things shall not be remembered or come to mind. But be glad and rejoice forever in what I am creating; for I am about to create Jerusalem as a joy, and its people as a delight. I will rejoice in Jerusalem, and delight in my people; no more shall the sound of weeping be heard in it, or the cry of distress."

42. Rev 21:12, 17—"It has a great, high wall with twelve gates, and at the gates twelve angels. . . . And he measured its wall, one hundred forty-four cubits, according to human measurements . . . and he measured the city with his rod, fifteen hundred miles."

43. Eph 2:1–3—"You were dead through the trespasses and sins in which you once lived, following the course of this world, following the ruler of the power of the air, the spirit that is now at work among those who are disobedient. All of us once lived among them in the passions of our flesh, following the desires of flesh and senses, and we were by nature

Issuing from the throne, the source of all life, is a constant and incorruptible supply of vitality, comfort, and blessing for God's people, symbolized by John's figure of a river of life.[44] They experience a never-ending and total satisfaction of all their glorified desires. John describes its sparkling brilliance as water which was as clear as crystal. By contrast, those who were not admitted to the city, have as their eternal abode the filthiest sewer imaginable, for it is in a place prepared for the devil and his angels.[45]

The population is fixed (it can neither increase nor decrease), and each inhabitant was personally chosen by God.[46] Together we continue to experience the endless depths of benefits and blessings which the omniscient, eternal, and omnipotent God has in store for those He called to Himself. Indeed there is no finalization or termination of our experience of God's infinite mercies and grace. What seemed at first to be perfect and unsurpassable, continues to grow richer, deeper, and more profound as the endless ages of eternity role on and on. Not only

---

children of wrath, like everyone else." Eph 2:12–13—"[R]emember that you were at that time without Christ, being aliens from the commonwealth of Israel, and strangers to the covenants of promise, having no hope and without God in the world. But now in Christ Jesus you who once were far off have been brought near by the blood of Christ."

44. Rev 22:1—see note 33.

45. Matt 25:41—"Then he will say to those at his left hand, 'You that are accursed, depart from me into the eternal fire prepared for the devil and his angels. . . .'" Rev 14:10—"[T]hey will also drink the wine of God's wrath, poured unmixed into the cup of his anger, and they will be tormented with fire and sulfur in the presence of the holy angels and in the presence of the Lamb."

46. Eph 1:4–6—"[J]ust as he chose us in Christ before the foundation of the world to be holy and blameless before him in love. He destined us for adoption as his children through Jesus Christ, according to the good pleasure of his will, to the praise of his glorious grace that he freely bestowed on us in the Beloved."

did God make all things new; He causes all things to continue to remain new for ever and ever. We continue to grow in our knowledge of God to ever-increasing heights of wonder and praise, far surpassing what previously seemed to be the ultimate and final point. What an experience to be developing on such an exalted trajectory but knowing the end will never be reached. But how satisfying, stimulating, and exalting are the steps along the way!

6

The Heavenly Environment

Eternity

DEAR _____,

Though the language of the former world really fails me, I still want to employ it to convey to you at least an inkling of the conditions in this new eternal world. Everywhere there is brightness (the former world seems to have been so dark by comparison), purity, and transparency; nothing is obscured by darkness or ignorance.[1] We bask in the endless expressions of the Creator's great liberty, variety, and symmetry. We are privileged

---

1. Rev 22:3—"And there shall be no more curse: but the throne of God and of the lamb shall be in it, and His servants shall serve Him: and they shall see his face, and His name shall be on their foreheads" (KJV). 1 Cor 13:12—"For now we see in a mirror, dimly, but then we will see face to face. Now I know only in part; then I will know fully, even as I have been fully known." 2 Pet 1:19—"So we have the prophetic message more fully confirmed. You will do well to be attentive to this as to a lamp shining in a dark place, until the day dawns and the morning star rises in your hearts."

to eat of the tree of life[2] and of the hidden manna;[3] we also wear upon us (being made worthy through the blood of the Lamb) God's very name, the name of His city, and the new name which He has given to us.[4]

Whatever God creates reflects His goodness and love, but in our glorified state we are much better able to perceive the expression of His perfections in the work of His hands. Certainly His eternal wisdom and power are displayed in much grander and more glorious ways in the new creation. There is an inexhaustible richness and wisdom in the ongoing operation of His providence. But in a sense it is frustrating for the finite mind because the more we observe of the activities prompted by His omniscience and brought about by his omnipotence, the more we realize that we really do not, and are unable to understand, that wisdom which brought the world into being, redeemed it, and brought it to its final consummation.[5] It boggles our minds

---

2. Rev 22:2—"On either side of the river is the tree of life with its twelve kinds of fruit, producing its fruit each month; and the leaves of the tree are for the healing of the nations." Rev 22:14—"Blessed are those who wash their robes, so that they will have the right to the tree of life and may enter the city by the gates."

3. Rev 2:17—"To everyone who conquers I will give some of the hidden manna, and I will give a white stone, and on the white stone is written a new name that no one knows except the one who receives it."

4. Rev 22:3—see note 1.

5. Ps 103:19—"The Lord has established his throne in the heavens; and His kingdom rules over all." Dan 4:35—"All the inhabitants of the earth are accounted as nothing, and he does what he wills with the host of heaven and the inhabitants of the earth. There is no one who can stay his hand or say to him, 'What are you doing?'" Acts 4:28—"to do whatever your hand and your plan had predestined to take place." Eph 1:9–10—"[H]e has made known to us the mystery of his will, according to his good pleasure that he set forth in Christ, as a plan for the fullness of time, to gather up all things in him, things in heaven and things on earth."

to think that our Creator had the whole process in mind before a single molecule was created. But as the ages of eternity wear on, we find ourselves ever reveling in a deeper and more profound appreciation of God's works, experiencing greater delight in Him and His works, and offering a more profound and exalted adoration and praise of Him who is the fountainhead of all true worth. His people offer continually, though still inadequately, the loudest anthems, the most rapturous hosannas, and the most ecstatic praises to Him who sits on the throne.

The joys of the older earth are far exceeded by the heavenly realities. In fact we are experiencing the joy of the Lord, unmixed and unending, in a way which we could have never imagined previously and which cannot be exaggerated. We now realize that the human authors of Holy Scripture were forced to use earthly language, with its great limitations, to explain realities which could not be fitted into categories of experience and conceptual grids of the previous world. We explore constantly that treasure house of things which on the former earth no eye could see, no ear could hear, and no heart could conceive.[6] We live in a world of inexpressible glory and bliss beyond anything we could have anticipated. With all of the effects of sin removed, we live in a world of incalculable blessings, beauty, and happiness. It is a world of perfect life and communion with both God and His people which provides for the enjoyment of loftier pleasures which are appropriate to this new order of existence. The upward spiral we experience has no limit; each new height which at

---

6. 1 Cor 2:9—"But, as it is written, 'What no eye has seen, nor ear heard, nor the human heart conceived, what God has prepared for those who love him. . . .'" Isa 65:17—"For I am about to create new heavens and a new earth; the former things shall not be remembered or come to mind."

first we think could not possibly be improved, becomes only the stepping stone to something loftier and more profound.[7]

When heaven was expanded to encompass the entire new creation, the very abode of God became our true and proper home as the people of God. We live as the family of God, we no longer relate to God by means of sacraments and symbols, and we are pleasured by the blessings He communicates and the joy He continues to dispense to His own throughout eternity. What a joy to fellowship with the innumerable hosts of the holy angels, to observe their carefully organized hierarchy,[8] to see them rejoicing over us,[9] to hear their penetrating questions about our experience of salvation,[10] and to be served by them.[11] I constantly wonder at the way I struggled with letting go of possessions and thrills of the former world when I had eternal

---

7. 1 Pet 1:8—"Although you have not seen him, you love him; and even though you do not see him now, you believe in him and rejoice with an indescribable and glorious joy. . . ."

8. Col 1:16—"[F]or in him all things in heaven and on earth were created, things visible and invisible, whether thrones or dominions or rulers or powers—all things have been created through him and for him. . . ." Eph 1:20–21—"God put this power to work in Christ when he raised him from the dead and seated him at his right hand in the heavenly places, far above all rule and authority and power and dominion, and above every name that is named, not only in this age but also in the age to come."

9. Luke 15:7—"Just so, I tell you, there will be more joy in heaven over one sinner who repents than over ninetynine righteous persons who need no repentance."

10. 1 Pet 1:12— "It was revealed to them that they were serving not themselves but you, in regard to the things that have now been announced to you through those who brought you good news by the Holy Spirit sent from heaven—things into which angels long to look!"

11. Heb 1:14—"Are not all angels spirits in the divine service, sent to serve for the sake of those who are to inherit salvation?"

delights awaiting me which totally dwarf all possible pleasures on the first earth. I have never heard any inhabitant of this new earth whisper even a sigh of longing for the previous world. The new is our permanent, totally satisfying, and eternal home.

This life of heaven is secure, unending, and guaranteed by the omnipotence and promise of the Almighty.[12] There is nothing to interrupt or lessen this blessed estate. There will be no intermission, eclipse, or overshadowing cloud throughout the endless ages of eternity.[13] Its population is stable in its number[14] and consistent in its exalted experiences of God's grace. Its members cannot outlive their happiness nor see it diminish through they do see it increase as God continues to lavish the riches of His grace upon them.

Though age is irrelevant and we sense no limitations or pressures imposed by the clock or the calendar as was true in the previous existence, time still exists in the sense of succession of events (time could be defined as the abstract possibility of then and now). We remember our first moment in this new creation and experience events ending and being replaced by others—we are certainly not eternal nor omnipresent as God is. Without time there would be no music to appreciate and to use in the

---

12. Matt 6:19–20—"Do not store up for yourselves treasures on earth, where moth and rust consume and where thieves break in and steal; but store up for yourselves treasures in heaven, where neither moth nor rust consumes and where thieves do not break in and steal. . . ."

13. Rev 21:4—"[H]e will wipe every tear from their eyes. Death will be no more; mourning and crying and pain will be no more, for the first things have passed away." Rev 21:27—"But nothing unclean will enter it, nor anyone who practices abomination or falsehood, but only those who are written in the Lamb's book of life."

14. John 20:27–28—"My sheep hear my voice. I know them, and they follow me. I give them eternal life, and they will never perish. No one will snatch them out of my hand."

worship and adoration of our Creator. Time is still a dimension of our creaturely existence, but it extends endlessly and forever.

In the recreation of the heavens and the earth God restored what was spoiled by the sin of the human race and returned to His people something so much better that it surpassed all of our earthly imaginations. Where there once was darkness and error, we live in the greatest light and truth; where there was enmity and hatred, now there is perfect love; where there was evil and sin, there is now perfect holiness. The heartbreaks and sorrows of the former world are not worthy of being compared with the glory which we are now experiencing.[15] God brought to full completion the redemption and perfection of his church and the happiness of His people. In fact, the church in the former world was only a faint shadow of its glorious eternal essence.

It is truly a world where the positives exist in perfection without what we once knew as the corresponding negatives. Where we once had to live by faith, now we live by sight. Where we once lived in a cursed world, now all traces of the former revolt, including the threats of the law and the curse for disobedience—death in all of its dreadful aspects and ramifications—have all been eliminated.[16] I have never seen a tear of sorrow shed for the millions of years I have enjoyed this heavenly paradise (we remember that our Savior took our griefs[17]).

---

15. Rom 8:18—"I consider that the sufferings of this present time are not worth comparing with the glory about to be revealed to us."

16. Rev 22:2–3—see notes 1 and 2. Rev 20:14—"Then Death and Hades were thrown into the lake of fire. This is the second death, the lake of fire. . . ."

17. Isa 53:4–6—"Surely he has borne our infirmities and carried our diseases; yet we accounted him stricken, struck down by God, and afflicted. But he was wounded for our transgressions, crushed for our iniquities; upon him was the punishment that made us whole, and by his bruises we are healed. All we like sheep have gone astray; we have all

It is a world where all is open and visible. It is a world without doctors, undertakers,[18] lawyers, orphans, homeless people, crisis centers, counseling services, decay, or disorder. It is a world without thieves,[19] locks or security systems, without weapons, and without fear of any kind.[20] Though we have responsibilities graciously given to us by our Creator,[21] by which to glorify Him, we no longer toil, earning our livelihood by the sweat of our brows. Everything is done with great joy without any burdens or pressures of any kind. There is no fear of failure, separation, or ostracism; in fact there are no worries of any kind. But above all, with the experience of being made perfect, there is no fear of being under God's displeasure and wrath. The Lamb forever absorbed in Himself, while on the cross, the eternal wrath of God which was due us so that none remains for us.[22] While the fire consumed the sacrifices in the Old Testament, when the Lamb of God was sacrificed at the cross, He Himself consumed the fire. Hallelujah!

---

turned to our own way, and the Lord has laid on him the iniquity of us all."

18. Rev 20:14—see note 16. It is significant in Scripture that nothing or no person ever returns from the lake of fire—there are no exceptions.

19. Matt 6:20—see note 12.

20. Rev 22:15—"Outside are the dogs and sorcerers and fornicators and murderers and idolaters, and everyone who loves and practices falsehood."

21. Matt 25:21—"His master said to him, 'Well done, good and trustworthy slave; you have been trustworthy in a few things, I will put you in charge of many things; enter into the joy of your master.'" Luke 16:11—"If then you have not been faithful with the dishonest wealth, who will entrust to you the true riches?"

22. Rom 8:1—"There is therefore now no condemnation for those who are in Christ Jesus."

In this new abode there are the loftiest heights of wisdom which we may explore and goodness which we may observe and practice, and there are inexhaustible treasures in unfathomable abysses of love to be experienced which have been brought into being by the infinitely creative, omniscient God whom we worship and adore. It is indescribable both being immersed in the most profound displays of the wisdom and being the beneficiaries of that intense and limitless love which is outside of any conceptual frameworks which we had ever previously possessed and growing in our knowledge of the One who is in Himself the ultimate and final reality. The most sublime heights of excellence lie before us, and we progress endlessly toward the infinite which is ahead. Everything we behold and experience is patterned after the image of God Himself.

One reality which is always part of our conscious worship is the wonder of God's grace. The contrast between what we deserve because of our original and our individual sins and what we have actually received from God's hand, is such that throughout all the endless ages of eternity we will never be able to offer sufficient gratitude and thanksgiving—we are eternal debtors to divine grace. Whatever we are and whatever we become, is due solely to God (no one brags in heaven[23]); it is our privilege to reflect His goodness and love. He remains the source of all love, affections, and tenderness. The superiority of this new order makes me appreciate all the more the wonder of the Incarnation; the eternal Son of God humbled Himself, putting

---

23. Eph 2:8–9—"For by grace you have been saved through faith, and this is not your own doing; it is the gift of God—not the result of works, so that no one may boast." 1 Cor 1:29–31—"[S]o that no one might boast in the presence of God. He is the source of your life in Christ Jesus, who became for us wisdom from God, and righteousness and sanctification and redemption, in order that, as it is written, 'Let the one who boasts, boast in the Lord.'"

aside the glories of heaven to assume a human nature in which he lived out a life of perfect obedience to God and died as a sinner in my place.[24]

In this environment we find ourselves constantly seeking new words to express the ever-growing exhilaration and joy we experience. When our experience far surpasses what we had previously defined as "joyful," "wonderful," and "amazing," we have to invent new ways for expressing and communicating those realities. Our experience has so outdistanced our vocabulary that we often do not even try to use words to describe the new plateaus of delight and ecstasy to which God brings us. What a thrill to experience pleasure without pain, joy with no sorrow, and security without threat.

Our condition as glorified human beings is truly blessed. We are joint-heirs with Christ,[25] and we reign with Him forever and ever.[26] It is amazing seeing fellow believers shining as the brightness of the expanse of heaven and like the stars forever and ever.[27] Indeed a day in the courts of heaven far surpasses an

---

24. Phil 2:6–8—"[W]ho, though he was in the form of God, did not regard equality with God as something to be exploited, but emptied himself, taking the form of a slave, being born in human likeness. And being found in human form, he humbled himself and became obedient to the point of death—even death on a cross." 2 Cor 5:21—"For our sake he made him to be sin who knew no sin, so that in him we might become the righteousness of God."

25. Rom 8:17—"[A]nd if children, then heirs, heirs of God and joint heirs with Christ—if, in fact, we suffer with him so that we may also be glorified with him."

26. Rev 3:21—"To the one who conquers I will give a place with me on my throne, just as I myself conquered and sat down with my Father on his throne." Rev 22:5—"[A]nd they will reign forever and ever."

27. Dan 12:3—"Those who are wise shall shine like the brightness of the sky, and those who lead many to righteousness, like the stars forever and ever."

eternity upon the earth.[28] We exist with the fullness of life and light, strength and youth; God's presence keeps everything vital and vigorous with fresh energy. It is glory added to glory, progressing constantly without end and with eternal life perfected. The glory of Christ which was prefigured in His transfiguration on earth[29] is now before our awestricken eyes constantly; it is our privilege to behold Him for ever without distraction or interruption and to be made like Him.[30] This heavenly existence affords perfect comfort and perfect pleasure, and far from being boring, it is more intriguing and captivating than we could have contemplated during our earthly sojourn.

What a thrill every time I eat anew of the tree of life with fellow inhabitants of the city and fall down and worship our Savior in person, not just by faith as was necessary in the previous world. In this world there is the great concert of innumerable voices singing with the greatest fervor and intensity in praise and thanksgiving to our common Creator and Redeemer. We live in consummate bliss with all of our energies and desires exercised now in a perfect life, which exudes all the communicable attributes of God which make up God-likeness. The former limitations are removed so that we may study the boundless universe

28. Ps 84:10—"For a day in your courts is better than a thousand elsewhere. I would rather be a doorkeeper in the house of my God than live in the tents of wickedness."

29. Matt 16:28—17:2—"'Truly I tell you, there are some standing here who will not taste death before they see the Son of Man coming in his kingdom.' Six days later, Jesus took with him Peter and James and his brother John and led them up a high mountain, by themselves. And he was transfigured before them, and his face shone like the sun, and his clothes became dazzling white." See also Mark 9:1–3.

30. 1 John 3:2—"What we do know is this: when he is revealed, we will be like him, for we will see him as he is." I Thess 4:17—"Then we who are alive, who are left, will be caught up in the clouds together with them to meet the Lord in the air; and so we will be with the Lord forever."

and be taught by the God-man throughout eternity without end or qualification.

In this new world the color spectrum is so much larger and broader, and our vision is able to take in so much more, both qualitatively and quantitatively, with the result that every moment the reality which surrounds us is perceived and appreciated with so much greater clarity, richness, and far deeper appreciation for the wisdom and omnipotence of our God. The range of sounds is also far greater and more refined than anything we had previously known, so we hear much more exquisitely and delicately the glorious sounds of this new order.

Thus the music in heaven is loftier and far more beautiful than anything we heard or could produce in the former world. It is also united in that everyone here has as his or her greatest motivation to exalt Jesus Christ. No musician hungers for personal recognition (and there are no copyrights) but desires only that Christ be worshiped and exalted. Every musician strives continually to find better, more skilled, and more appropriate ways to express gratitude and praise to the Lamb that was slain and for the incomparable God and Father of our Lord Jesus Christ. Life in heaven is a constant, fervent, and an ever-improving experience of doxology.[31]

---

31. Rev 5:9–14—"They sing a new song: 'You are worthy to take the scroll and to open its seals, for you were slaughtered and by your blood you ransomed for God saints from every tribe and language and people and nation; you have made them to be a kingdom and priests serving our God, and they will reign on earth.' Then I looked, and I heard the voice of many angels surrounding the throne and the living creatures and the elders; they numbered myriads of myriads and thousands of thousands, singing with full voice, 'Worthy is the Lamb that was slaughtered to receive power and wealth and wisdom and might and honor and glory and blessing!' Then I heard every creature in heaven and on earth and under the earth and in the sea, and all that is in them, singing, 'To the one seated on the throne and to the Lamb be blessing and honor and glory

In contrast to this indescribably blessed estate of the redeemed, is the awful judgment of the wicked. Those whose mortal life ended without a saving union with Jesus Christ, are suffering the undiluted wrath of God in the lake of fire and brimstone.[32] As their hatred of God and cursing of His name continues, their punishment increases with ever more ferocity and intensity so that their eternal debt is increased and multiplied over and over again. But that terrible suffering in no way detracts from the bliss and glory of the existence of the saints with Christ their Lord. Two passages which often came to mind in the transition from the mortal to the immortal life were:

> You will only look with your eyes and see the punishment of the wicked. Ps 91:8

> For God has destined us not for wrath but for obtaining salvation through our Lord Jesus Christ. . . . 1 Thess 5:9

In fact we no longer feel any tenderness or compassion toward the lost as we did in the old order. The redeemed are so taken up in praise and wonder at the purposes and perfections of God, that they praise Him for His wrath which is executed on those He has designated as proper objects of that eternal wrath.[33]

---

and might forever and ever!' And the four living creatures said, 'Amen!' And the elders fell down and worshiped."

32. Rev 14:9–11—"Those who worship the beast and its image, and receive a mark on their foreheads or on their hands, they will also drink the wine of God's wrath, poured unmixed into the cup of his anger, and they will be tormented with fire and sulfur in the presence of the holy angels and in the presence of the Lamb. And the smoke of their torment goes up forever and ever. There is no rest day or night for those who worship the beast and its image and for anyone who receives the mark of its name." See also Rev 20:15.

33. Rev 19:1–4—"After this I heard what seemed to be the loud voice of a great multitude in heaven, saying, 'Hallelujah! Salvation and

They glory in His justice and holiness which are vindicated in the eternal punishment of those who have violated His character and broken His law. The redeemed now love only what Jesus loves and wants them to love, what honors Him, and reflects His likeness. The suffering of the wicked (Rev 14:11) is a constant reminder of the depths of God's love and grace to the saints and intensifies their praise and thanksgiving toward God for His unmerited favor and goodness to them.

---

glory and power to our God, for his judgments are true and just; he has judged the great whore who corrupted the earth with her fornication, and he has avenged on her the blood of his servants.' Once more they said, 'Hallelujah! The smoke goes up from her forever and ever.' And the twentyfour elders and the four living creatures fell down and worshiped God who is seated on the throne, saying, 'Amen. Hallelujah!'"

7

The Personal Dimension

Eternity

D^{EAR} ,

We are now exactly what and whom God created us to be. What a thrill to discover finally and unchangeably who we are and to be exactly what God destined us to be and in the place he has designed for us from all eternity. Only here in God's presence is there the perfect unfolding and expression of each human personality. In this city each personality attains its full maturity and each person discovers his or her own identity and uniqueness in terms of the new name which God has granted to each.[1] Human nature is now elevated to the highest possible plateau, a height which was unthinkable in the previous existence.[2] It is exalted in this kingdom prepared for mankind from the beginning. The creativity implanted within each person is now afforded the opportunity for the fullest expression and development in ways which glorify and exalt the Most High

---

1. Rev 2:17—"To everyone who conquers I will give some of the hidden manna, and I will give a white stone, and on the white stone is written a new name that no one knows except the one who receives it."

2. Rom 8:17—"[I]f, in fact, we suffer with him so that we may also be glorified with him." Rom 8:30—"and those whom he justified he also glorified."

God. The Creator has taken each redeemed son of Adam and exquisitely tailored him or her for the bliss of the eternal state. With the ability to sin removed forever[3] and the highest degree of personal perfection achieved in both body and soul, there is nothing to thwart or hinder the fulfillment of the enormous potential within each person. Heaven is filled with people who are involved in glorious actions, great enjoyment, spontaneous laughter, and continual celebration. The soul rests in God fully and perfectly, experiencing His infinite love and grace, and rejoices in Him; its chief good is the enjoyment of God Himself.[4] In this relationship there flows the experience of full and eternally uninterrupted peace.[5]

Through the process of death, the intermediate state, then resurrection and glorification, our personalities, memories, and history of relationships all remained the same. Our individuality was preserved in the same way that Moses and Elijah maintained their identities on the Mount of Transfiguration;[6] we have our same earthly body though now in its glorified state.[7] We are

---

3. Heb 12:22–23—"But you have come to Mount Zion and to the city of the living God, the heavenly Jerusalem, and to innumerable angels in festal gathering, and to the assembly of the firstborn who are enrolled in heaven, and to God the judge of all, and to the spirits of the righteous made perfect. . . ."

4. Ps 118:14—"The Lord is my strength and my might; he has become my salvation." See also Exod 15:2 and Isaiah 12:2.

5. John 14:27—"Peace I leave with you; my peace I give to you. I do not give to you as the world gives. Do not let your hearts be troubled, and do not let them be afraid." Rom 14:17—"For the kingdom of God is not food and drink but righteousness and peace and joy in the Holy Spirit."

6. Matt 17:2–3—"And he was transfigured before them, and his face shone like the sun, and his clothes became dazzling white. Suddenly there appeared to them Moses and Elijah, talking with him."

7. 1 Cor 15:52–53—"[I]n a moment, in the twinkling of an eye, at the last trumpet. For the trumpet will sound, and the dead will be raised

forever who we were (our selfhood remains), but on this side of eternity all moral and physical blemishes have been removed. We recognize one another readily; in fact, those we comforted, assisted, and ministered to, welcomed us into this new home and continue to be grateful for our service to them. One fellow saint told me that a particular lesson I had taught from Scripture proved to be a real turning point in his life; I remembered the day because I felt so miserable; it was only divine grace which enabled me to teach at all that day. Another person thanked me for giving him what I had on one occasion; I was so embarrassed because it was so little, but in an amazing way the Master took that little bit and multiplied it exceedingly as He did with the loaves and fishes of the little boy.[8] We also know other saints with a greater fullness and accuracy than was possible in the mortal life. Identification of our racial, tribal, and national identities remain (though without rivalry or enmity) both as an affirmation of the continuation of personality and identity and as an object of praise to the Redeemer who bought people with His own blood from "every tribe and tongue and people and nation."[9] Since gender is part of our individuality, this aspect of our personality remains (we are not androgynous) though the

---

imperishable, and we will be changed. For this perishable body must put on imperishability, and this mortal body must put on immortality."

8. Matt 14:13–21.

9. Rev 5:9—"They sing a new song: 'You are worthy to take the scroll and to open its seals, for you were slaughtered and by your blood you ransomed for God saints from every tribe and language and people and nation.'" Rev 7:9—"After this I looked, and there was a great multitude that no one could count, from every nation, from all tribes and peoples and languages, standing before the throne and before the Lamb, robed in white, with palm branches in their hands."

exclusiveness of marriage and its reproductive potential are no longer part of our being.[10]

This deep, fulfilling, and indescribable relationship with God also has very profound effects on the saints' horizontal relationships. While marriage between a man and a woman (and sexual activity) no longer exists (e.g., there is no need for procreation, for protection of the woman, for a specific help-meet, and for sexual relief), the benefits of this creation ordinance are now seen to be only dim intimations of the greater delights which our Creator has established for our eternal relationships. Godly human marriages pointed to the great marriage supper of the Lamb[11] where the godly were perfectly assimilated into that great union of the Lamb with His bride.[12] They were pointers and small, but imperfect, pictures in the first world of that great marriage at which the eternal blessedness of God's people was launched in its visible form. In the eternal, loving union with Christ, all of the deepest needs of the human soul are being satisfied to the full, including the desire for relational intimacy.

---

10. Matt 22:30—"For in the resurrection they neither marry nor are given in marriage, but are like angels in heaven."

11. Rev 19:9—"Blessed are those who are invited to the marriage supper of the Lamb."

12. Rev 21:9–10—"'Come, I will show you the bride, the wife of the Lamb.' And in the spirit he carried me away to a great, high mountain and showed me the holy city Jerusalem coming down out of heaven from God." Eph 5:28–32—"In the same way, husbands should love their wives as they do their own bodies. He who loves his wife loves himself. For no one ever hates his own body, but he nourishes and tenderly cares for it, just as Christ does for the church, because we are members of his body. 'For this reason a man will leave his father and mother and be joined to his wife, and the two will become one flesh.' This is a great mystery, and I am applying it to Christ and the church."

Though Scripture gave us some whispered hints about the nature of the resurrection body,[13] its nature remained a mystery to us until we met Christ in the air[14] and received our eternal dwelling.[15] We were then made conformable to the body of His glory by the working of His omnipotence.[16] His resurrected and glorified body was the pattern and model of our resurrected bodies. This spiritual body is totally subordinate to the will and designs of God for our eternal existence, and out of this now perfect temple of God shines a dazzling luster, a beauty and a glory which is incorruptible and heavenly. If we had been allowed to view even the least of the glorified saints

13. 1 Cor 15:42–49—"So it is with the resurrection of the dead. What is sown is perishable, what is raised is imperishable. It is sown in dishonor, it is raised in glory. It is sown in weakness, it is raised in power. It is sown a physical body, it is raised a spiritual body. If there is a physical body, there is also a spiritual body. Thus it is written, 'The first man, Adam, became a living being'; the last Adam became a lifegiving spirit. But it is not the spiritual that is first, but the physical, and then the spiritual. The first man was from the earth, a man of dust; the second man is from heaven. As was the man of dust, so are those who are of the dust; and as is the man of heaven, so are those who are of heaven. Just as we have borne the image of the man of dust, we will also bear the image of the man of heaven."

14. 1 Thess 4:16–17—"For the Lord himself, with a cry of command, with the archangel's call and with the sound of God's trumpet, will descend from heaven, and the dead in Christ will rise first. Then we who are alive, who are left, will be caught up in the clouds together with them to meet the Lord in the air; and so we will be with the Lord forever."

15. 2 Cor 5:1—"For we know that if the earthly tent we live in is destroyed, we have a building from God, a house not made with hands, eternal in the heavens."

16. Phil 3:20–21—"But our citizenship is in heaven, and it is from there that we are expecting a Savior, the Lord Jesus Christ. He will transform the body of our humiliation that it may be conformed to the body of his glory, by the power that also enables him to make all things subject to himself."

during our mortal sojourn, we would have instinctively (but wrongly) fallen down to worship such a resplendent sight. Both body and soul, in perfect harmony, were made to participate in this consummated union with the glorified Christ. The faces of the redeemed were beautified and likened after Christ Himself in glorified bodies which are exquisite and incomparable to anything in the former world.

As God caused the acorn to become an oak tree and the caterpillar a butterfly, so the omnipotent and all-gracious Creator took our mortal bodies, redeemed them, raised them, and gave them the eternal structure which would best reflect His purposes and intentions. The wisdom and power of God in this recreative process left us in absolute astonishment. Now the divine likeness which is expressed in the love and the holiness of the inner man, is made perfect and shines externally throughout the outward body that the redeemed might reflect the character of God in a perfect fashion.[17] The glorified body is a spiritual body,[18] one that can better express the inner aspirations which are part of the new birth and which can fulfill man's true spiritual nature. It is also celestial in that it is fitted for our heavenly existence.[19] This body serves perfectly the needs of the glorified soul; it allows us to love God with the totality of our beings. It is not only incorruptible,[20] but it also has a continual freshness and vigor which is incapable of decay or weakness.[21] No longer is our relationship with God affected adversely by physical or

---

17. 1 Cor 15:49—see note 13.

18. 1 Cor 15:44—see note 13.

19. 1 Cor 15:40—"There are both heavenly bodies and earthly bodies, but the glory of the heavenly is one thing, and that of the earthly is another." 1 Cor 15:49—see note 13.

20. 1 Cor 15:53—see note 7.

21. 1Cor 15:43—see note 13.

emotional weaknesses. The constant vitality of the body means that we no longer have to be careful to guard our physical, emotional, and psychological output (maintaining a necessary reserve) to prevent burnout, breakdowns, or emptiness. We can give to one another out of ever-replenishing strength and vigor supplied by our omnipresent and all-gracious Creator (we are reminded of the widow's jar of oil in Elijah's time).[22] This glorious body far surpasses the frail earthen tabernacle which served us well in the temporary mortal life even with its weaknesses. It shows the wisdom and power of God in a far more profound and comprehensive way than our former vessel could ever do. The donning of this glorified body was an experience of incalculable triumph and exaltation as we were given a body fitted for the new heavens and the new earth, one which is appropriate to the growth, progress, and worship of the new age and through which we can experience the joy of uninterrupted, unclouded, and unhindered fellowship with the triune God.

The new bodies we received are forever perfect, with radiant beauty and brilliant splendor which outshines the former sun and stars.[23] They are perfectly fitted for the eternal, heavenly existence; the body and mind are marvelously coordinated so that the outer frame corresponds completely with the inner soul which is perfected in godliness. This is no longer a dissonance between our glorious position in Christ and our daily walk. We are indeed now the perfect temple for the full indwelling and absolute empowering of the Holy Spirit. We have been transformed fully into the image of the Lord in the most glorious

---

22. 1 Kgs 17:16—"The jar of meal was not emptied, neither did the jug of oil fail, according to the word of the Lord that he spoke by Elijah."

23. Dan 12:3—"Those who are wise shall shine like the brightness of the sky, and those who lead many to righteousness, like the stars for ever and ever."

manner[24]; where we once bore the image of the earthly, we now bear forever and unchangeably the image of the heavenly.[25]

Our souls have had all the vestiges of corruption and depravity removed so that where there was once meanness, there is kindness; where there was pride, there is deep and sincere humility; where there was self-seeking, now there is a total self-giving disposition; where there was materialism and idolatry, there is the absolute and unhindered worship of the Almighty. Where there was once self-exaltation, in its place there is self-abasement, a longing that Christ be exalted and worshiped. Our old nature ("the flesh") exists no longer in our glorified existence[26] so there are no internal points of sensitivity to temptation, and of course there are no more external sources of temptation since "the world" has been destroyed,[27] and the devil and his angels are experiencing external destruction and absolute and eternal separation from the godly.[28] No longer are there struggles with such vices ("deadly sins") as selfishness, unbelief, pride, covetousness, lust (carnal desires and evil passions), and anxiety. We

---

24. 2 Cor 3:18—"And all of us, with unveiled faces, seeing the glory of the Lord as though reflected in a mirror, are being transformed into the same image from one degree of glory to another; for this comes from the Lord, the Spirit."

25. 1 Cor 15:49—see note 13.

26. Heb 12:23—see note 3.

27. 1 John 2:16–17—"[F]or all that is in the world—the desire of the flesh, the desire of the eyes, the pride in riches—comes not from the Father but from the world. And the world and its desire are passing away, but those who do the will of God live for ever."

28. Jude 6; 2 Pet 2:4—"For if God did not spare the angels when they sinned, but cast them into hell and committed them to chains of deepest darkness to be kept until the judgment . . ." Rev 20:10—"And the devil who had deceived them was thrown into the lake of fire and sulphur, where the beast and the false prophet were, and they will be tormented day and night for ever and ever."

experience no cold hearts, no lukewarmness; we know no selfish or unwholesome desires; in fact all traces of fallenness have been removed from us (the only traces of the fallen world which remain are the scars on our Saviour's glorified body). No defect remains in the will and we live above even the most remote possibility of sinning. God has given us a new capacity so that we delight in doing the will of Christ. What an amazing sense of freedom to be able only to do the will of God, and no more even to have the ability to sin. I have neither sinned nor witnessed a single sin since God in His mercy brought me to this glorified state millions of years ago.

Our wills are now made one with God's so that we need no restraints or threats to motivate us toward godliness. This renovation of the soul means that we always do what we ought to do—our duty (which is our highest joy) and our practice are always the same. Our souls are disposed to every holy exercise; every aspiration or intention is directed toward the glory of God as well as the good of others and ourselves. We can both give and receive love with a depth, freedom, sincerity, and utter selflessness that we had never experienced in the previous world. The pleasures of heaven stretch our glorified sensibilities to their breaking point.

Having this total purification in heart, soul, and mind, we also experience wholeness as persons which always eluded us in the previous life. In our thanksgiving to God we are often mindful of the great change we have undergone from vile sinners under His wrath and condemnation to the present position of joint heirs with Christ and shining as the brightness of the firmament forever and ever. All the disfigurements on the bride of Christ have been removed, and there are no more associations with defiling agents.[29]

---

29. Rev 21:27—"But nothing unclean will enter it, nor anyone who

In this world most of the talents and gifts possessed on earth are improved, refined, and given the opportunity for perfect expression (the gift of evangelism is an exception since winning souls to Christ was only possible in the former world). Some, such as pastoring and mercy, are expressed in quite different ways but are nonetheless present. No glorified person experiences frustration over possessing gifts for which there appears to be no appropriate context for expression or use. There is also the satisfaction of intellectual inquiry, the delighting of the aesthetic senses, and the fulfillment of all holy ideals.

We continuously receive from the endless superabundance of Christ's riches and advance more in union and consolidation with Him who is our Head and Lord. He is forever active in communicating the blessings of the heavenly existence to His own. The salvation, which is ours in Christ, is an eternal wonder, and as we on earth received "grace upon grace,"[30] so now the constantly renewed expressions of grace leave us enraptured and astonished. We remember so well the powerful, sovereign working of divine grace in our lives in the mortal sphere and marvel that our sins, put under the blood of Christ, are not remembered and are never brought before us in any way. How marvelous it is to be experiencing the continual fulfillment of Paul's prayer, "[T]hat you, being rooted and grounded in love, may be able to comprehend with all the saints what is the breadth and length and height and depth, and to know the love of Christ which surpasses knowledge, that you may be filled up to all the fullness of God."[31]

---

practices abomination or falsehood, but only those who are written in the Lamb's book of life."

30. John 1:16—"From his fullness we have all received, grace upon grace."

31. Eph 3:17–21.

In this heavenly world God's will is carried out instantly, completely, and joyously.[32] Indeed Christ has reigned in an uncontested manner ever since His coronation as the absolute and universal sovereign over all things.[33] How my heart rejoices that sin is only a distant memory from the past. In fact it is one of those words which we never use in our heavenly vocabulary, along with "death," "decay," "disobedience," "suffering," "pain," and "sorrow."[34] Because there is no reality to which they correspond or represent, such words have no place in our heavenly dictionary.

Our desires are perfectly pure, our previously imperfect thoughts are now corrected and/or eclipsed, and our mind elevated and filled with glorious thoughts appropriate to the new creation. The glorified soul is granted higher senses of perception and understanding of created reality and of God the Uncreated. Because of Christ's atoning work, which has now been consummated, we are made pure in both body and soul so that now we live, move, and breathe in the atmosphere of perfect holiness. In this complete sanctification we experience an ever-increasing and indescribably rich delight in the infinite depths of God's being.

---

32. Matt 6:10—"Your kingdom come. Your will be done, on earth as it is in heaven."

33. Phil 2:10–11—"[S]o that at the name of Jesus every knee should bend, in heaven and on earth and under the earth, and every tongue should confess that Jesus Christ is Lord, to the glory of God the Father." Rev 19:16—"On his robe and on his thigh he has a name inscribed, 'King of kings and Lord of lords.'"

34. Rev 20:14—"Then Death and Hades were thrown into the lake of fire. This is the second death, the lake of fire." Rev 21:4—"[H]e will wipe every tear from their eyes. Death will be no more; mourning and crying and pain will be no more, for the first things have passed away."

We now are immersed in an overflowing, even ravishing and immeasurable, fullness of life[35] which dwarfs all previous joys in the mortal life. In this atmosphere of God's perfect, undiluted, and inexhaustible joy, our affections are truly blessed; in fact, with nothing to cool, rival, or divert our affections for God, they are infinitely inflamed and now burn with untiring energy and power. We love God wholeheartedly and others most sincerely with the greatest ardor of affection and serve God with the most passionate flame of pure devotion and holy zeal. We love each other as Christ loves us and we see in each of our fellow saints the beauty of Christ reflected in a unique way.

It is as though the godly are swallowed up in the inexhaustible ocean of divine love and blessedness, bathed in His uncreated light, and eternally reflecting that light and love toward God which is the truest possible self love. No language can articulate what it is like to be embraced by a love that is divine, eternal, and perfect.[36] But the godly enter moment-by-moment into that very experience.

---

35. That which we experience in heaven is beyond happiness, joy, and even exhilaration. It is an exuberance that comes from delight in the Creator and gratitude for His marvelous works along with a sense of not having sufficient capacity to receive the vastness of His love and mercy. It is an experience of being totally enraptured, overcome by His goodness and grace. 1 Pet 1:8 ("Although you have not seen him, you love him; and even though you do not see him now, you believe in him and rejoice with an indescribable and glorious joy. . . .") expresses the first fruits of this great joy which we began to experience in the former world, but is now brought to previously unimaginable heights in the eternal world.

36. Jer 31:3—"[T]he Lord appeared to him from far away. I have loved you with an everlasting love; therefore I have continued my faithfulness to you." Rom 8:38–39—"For I am convinced that neither death, nor life, nor angels, nor rulers, nor things present, nor things to come, nor powers, nor height, nor depth, nor anything else in all creation, will be able to separate us from the love of God in Christ Jesus our Lord." 1 John

The longings, aspirations, and holy desires of the human heart, mind, and soul are filled to overflowing. Talents are developed, tastes are satisfied, holy affections are aroused, aesthetic instincts are given grand expression, and lofty ideals are realized. Individual strength is constantly renewed by the bread of life,[37] the water of life, and the tree of life.[38] The glorified saints live in absolute and perfect comfort. Every necessity is met with immediate and full supply.[39]

Within this heavenly existence there are vivid memories of the wonder and power of God's sovereign grace which drew us effectually to Himself and maintained us in that realm of grace amidst the temptations and stumbling blocks which were so ever present in the fallen world. The remembrance of this conquering and indomitable grace ever propels us to renew the presentation of ourselves to God for His service in the new world. With the canceling of the curse,[40] we know no fatigue or weariness, no pain or suffering, and no sorrow or bereavement. In fact, we are encouraged to eat freely and regularly from the

---

4:10—"Herein is love, not that we loved God, but that he loved us, and sent his Son to be the propitiation for our sins" (KJV).

37. John 6:48–51—"I am the bread of life. Your ancestors ate the manna in the wilderness, and they died. This is the bread that comes down from heaven, so that one may eat of it and not die. I am the living bread that came down from heaven. Whoever eats of this bread will live forever; and the bread that I will give for the life of the world is my flesh. . . ."

38. Rev 22:1–2—"Then the angel showed me the river of the water of life, bright as crystal, flowing from the throne of God and of the Lamb through the middle of the street of the city. On either side of the river is the tree of life with its twelve kinds of fruit, producing its fruit each month; and the leaves of the tree are for the healing of the nations."

39. Rom 8:32—"He who did not withhold his own Son, but gave him up for all of us, will he not with him also give us everything else?"

40. Rev 22:3—"And there shall be no more curse" (KJV).

tree of life with all of its healing powers; thus we live in optimal health perpetually. We, furthermore, encounter no hindrances in the pursuit of holiness and no distractions from the pursuit of all that is holy, righteous, and good. All limitations in the development of godliness have been removed. Though we have responsibilities graciously given to us by our Creator, by which to glorify Him, we no longer toil, earning our livelihood by the sweat of our brows.

The perfection of this new existence does not in any way nullify progress. Eternal life is not only unending, but it is also always increasing in its richness and intensity. There is growth in the enjoyment of God, of fellowship with Him, and there is growth in ways of serving Him and fellow saints. There is growth in the appreciation and understanding of God's creative work and in understanding the all-encompassing atoning work of Jesus Christ. In this world there are no limits or boundaries, only beginnings. Rather than finality, we experience advancement from glory to glory, from grace to greater grace. I have found more and more the richest delight, in an ever-increasing measure, in penetrating more into the inexhaustible depths of God Himself (we know Him accurately though never exhaustively). The more I grow in this knowledge of Him the greater the hunger and thirst to know Him more deeply. Eternal blessedness is continually accelerating with ever brightening prospects for the future. No one has ever felt that the glories of heaven have been exhausted so that monotony has set in. Rather there is a continual awe at how much more there is yet to experience. The capacities of the blessed are made to increase so that there are greater degrees of pleasure and happiness that are possible as the ages of eternity roll on. The continuing growth in knowledge and truth is most stimulating; the spirit within truly is overjoyed at the prospect of ceaseless development and greater attainment in what is true and holy. There is also progress in the appreciation of the infinite love of Christ and its implications for us in learning how both to give and to receive love. With the greater and greater thirst for the things of God are ever-increasing rivers of life gushing from the throne of God to satisfy that thirst and to bring it to even greater desire.

A place where great progress also continues to take place is in our spiritual understanding. We now have a much clearer understanding, as Scripture foretold[41]; we have a heightened capacity to understand matters which previously were far beyond our abilities and to perceive far more adequately many matters which we could only faintly discern. Our present knowledge totally dwarfs even what used to be our most profound understanding of divine truths. Many mysteries have been untangled for us in the heavenly school, and we understand now in a much more profound way how God in His grace and infinite wisdom had a definite end in everything that happened to us in the earthly sphere, even in those occurrences and circumstances that seemed to be so arbitrary and purposeless. All events, from the most momentous to the most seemingly trivial, were all woven so skillfully and wisely by the God who makes all things work together for the good of those who love Him.[42] The intricacy, comprehensiveness, and depth of His wise purposes and acts leave us absolutely spellbound in contemplating their design on this side of eternity. In the light of the reality of glorification we better perceive something of why our Creator brought us into being and why He chose each of the redeemed out of the fallen

---

41. 1 Cor 13:12—"For now we see in a mirror, dimly, but then we will see face to face. Now I know only in part; then I will know fully, even as I have been fully known."

42. Rom 8:28—"We know that all things work together for good for those who love God, who are called according to his purpose."

mass of humanity.[43] We also have greater insight into why many specific trials and sufferings, so painful and troubling at the time, were ordered for our individual lives. Even those circumstances for which I could see no good or purpose at the time, I now know were brought about by the infinite love and wisdom of God. It was part of His tender grooming and pruning of me to make me what He wanted me to be.[44] How intimately He knew me[45] and exactly He determined what I needed in order

43. Eph 1:4–6—"[J]ust as he chose us in Christ before the foundation of the world to be holy and blameless before him in love. He destined us for adoption as his children through Jesus Christ, according to the good pleasure of his will, to the praise of his glorious grace that he freely bestowed on us in the Beloved." Rom 8:29–30—"For those whom he foreknew he also predestined to be conformed to the image of his Son, in order that he might be the firstborn within a large family. And those whom he predestined he also called; and those whom he called he also justified; and those whom he justified he also glorified."

44. Jas 1:2–4—"My brothers and sisters, whenever you face trials of any kind, consider it nothing but joy, because you know that the testing of your faith produces endurance; and let endurance have its full effect, so that you may be mature and complete, lacking in nothing." 1 Pet 1:6–7—"In this you rejoice, even if now for a little while you have had to suffer various trials, so that the genuineness of your faith—being more precious than gold that, though perishable, is tested by fire—may be found to result in praise and glory and honor when Jesus Christ is revealed."

45. Ps 139:13–18—"For it was you who formed my inward parts; you knit me together in my mother's womb. I praise you, for I am fearfully and wonderfully made. Wonderful are your works; that I know very well. My frame was not hidden from you, when I was being made in secret, intricately woven in the depths of the earth. Your eyes beheld my unformed substance. In your book were written all the days that were formed for me, when none of them as yet existed. How weighty to me are your thoughts, O God! How vast is the sum of them! I try to count them—they are more than the sand; I come to the end—I am still with you." Isa 49:15–16—"Can a woman forget her nursing child, or show

to be brought into greater conformity with Christ. The final result which He has brought about, by far outweighs whatever temporary inconvenience or pain I may have experienced.[46] It is also true that we can see so many of the details of history in an entirely different perspective now that the whole picture is before us and the Sovereign God's final result is made known.

This blessed increase in the understanding of the ways and acts of God in no way means that the redeemed (or the holy angels for that matter) have ever or will ever attain unto omniscience. Only God Himself has the total, absolute knowledge of all things,[47] and I often have the sense that no matter how my knowledge of Him and His ways increases, my understanding will only remain superficial at best. The more I know of God Almighty, the greater is my sense of ignorance and the greater

---

no compassion for the child of her womb? Even these may forget, yet I will not forget you. See, I have inscribed you on the palms of my hands; your walls are continually before me." Matt 10:29–31—"Are not two sparrows sold for a penny? Yet not one of them will fall to the ground apart from your Father. And even the hairs of your head are all counted. So do not be afraid; you are of more value than many sparrows." 1 Cor 13:12—"Now I know only in part; then I will know fully, even as I have been fully known."

46. 2 Cor 4:17—"For this slight momentary affliction is preparing us for an eternal weight of glory beyond all measure. . . ."

47. Isa 40:13–14—"Who has directed the spirit of the Lord, or as his counselor has instructed him? Whom did he consult for his enlightenment, and who taught him the path of justice? Who taught him knowledge, and showed him the way of understanding?" Rom 11:33–36—"O the depth of the riches and wisdom and knowledge of God! How unsearchable are his judgments and how inscrutable his ways! 'For who has known the mind of the Lord? Or who has been his counselor?' 'Or who has given a gift to him, to receive a gift in return?' For from him and through him and to him are all things. To him be the glory forever. Amen." 1 Cor 2:16—"For who has known the mind of the Lord so as to instruct him? . . ."

the Subject Matter seems to grow (although obviously that which is immutable cannot increase). The increase in our knowledge[48] (which is not diminished by forgetfulness nor age as in the previous world) heightens the adoration and praise, which I render to God. The attributes and perfections of God are more and more being unveiled to my wondering eyes. And since His attributes require a context for their revelation to mortal creatures, God has provided new contexts in which attributes are revealed to us as saints that we had no framework for considering while we were in the previous existence. How marvelous to think that He will be revealing new attributes to us throughout all eternity as well as new insights into attributes that we have already come to know. Indeed theology books have to be open-ended in this world. The great creeds and confessions of the previous order, though true, now seem to be so infantile in their expression of the truths concerning the God who is infinite, eternal, and unchangeable.

---

48. Eph 2:7—"[S]o that in the ages to come he might show the immeasurable riches of his grace in kindness toward us in Christ Jesus."

8

The Social Relationships

Eternity

D<small>EAR</small> ,

In this eternal state our union with Christ is enjoyed and apprehended apart from the effects of sin (on the body, the soul, and the mind) which we previously experienced and which kept us from fully understanding and rejoicing in that glorious relationship with the lover of our souls. We have been conformed to His image in holiness and righteousness[1] and are more and more closely united with Him who embodies absolute perfection and the absolute good. The glory of God fills the whole soul, and the light of Christ shines upon each redeemed person, enabling him or her to reflect the likeness of Christ in a distinct and unique way.

Being joined with Christ also brought us into membership with His body which contains the best men and women of all times, the nobility of the universe, those chosen before the foundation of the earth by the omniscient God to be in the

---

1. 2 Cor 3:18—"And all of us, with unveiled faces, seeing the glory of the Lord as though reflected in a mirror, are being transformed into the same image from one degree of glory to another; for this comes from the Lord, the Spirit." Rom 8:29—"For those whom he foreknew he also predestined to be conformed to the image of his Son, in order that he might be the firstborn within a large family."

Beloved Son.[2] All the innumerable multitudes of the redeemed from all times, places, and peoples, form one great communion and fellowship under Christ the Head.[3] The communion with fellow believers is deeper and richer than any human relationships which were ever possible in the mortal sphere. What a joy to continue to get to know those who were our fellow travelers and are now our intimate companions throughout all eternity. The human dimension is heightened and intensified by the presence of Christ who, as God, truly is the fountain of love, and, as man, knows the true human experience.

In spite of our total unworthiness we have been invited to share the honor and glory of heaven, and we have had our deepest sense of estrangement and pain removed forever. At last we are fully a part of that kingdom from which we often felt so distanced in the previous world, though we accepted membership by faith from the time of our conversion.[4] It hit me with

---

2. Eph 1:4–5—". . . just as he chose us in Christ before the foundation of the world to be holy and blameless before him in love. He destined us for adoption as his children through Jesus Christ, according to the good pleasure of his will."

3. Eph 4:4–5—"There is one body and one Spirit, just as you were called to the one hope of your calling, one Lord, one faith, one baptism. . . ." Rom 12:4–5—"For as in one body we have many members, and not all the members have the same function, so we, who are many, are one body in Christ, and individually we are members one of another." Rev 5:9–10—"They sing a new song: 'You are worthy to take the scroll and to open its seals, for you were slaughtered and by your blood you ransomed for God saints from every tribe and language and people and nation; you have made them to be a kingdom and priests serving our God, and they will reign on earth.'"

4. Eph 2:19–20—"So then you are no longer strangers and aliens, but you are citizens with the saints and also members of the household of God, built upon the foundation of the apostles and prophets, with Christ Jesus himself as the cornerstone." Rom 8:16–17—"it is that very

unimaginable joy when I realized that I was part of the church which is Christ's body and which He has claimed as His bride.

The love between individuals is now of a much more intense quality and is capable of being expressed much more widely and deeply than in the previous world. There are perfect affections between human beings from diverse backgrounds, places, temperaments, and callings. People are able and willing to give to one another their time, their energy, and their attention with reckless abandonment. Human relationships in the glorified state are deep and fully satisfying; in fact the redeemed person is capable of enjoying a deep and perfect relationship with every individual he encounters. We feel so close to one another, but never crowded, and communication is both immediate and perfect. This communion and fellowship exists between all branches of redeemed humanity, no matter what the respective stations may have been in the previous world, so that slaves and kings, the rich and the poor, and the most educated and the most uneducated, all live in a relationship of reciprocal love and sharing. There are no class distinctions in this new order.[5]

Spirit bearing witness with our spirit that we are children of God, and if children, then heirs, heirs of God and joint heirs with Christ—if, in fact, we suffer with him so that we may also be glorified with him."

5. Gal 3:28—"There is no longer Jew or Greek, there is no longer slave or free, there is no longer male and female; for all of you are one in Christ Jesus." Eph 2:12–16—"[R]emember that you were at that time without Christ, being aliens from the commonwealth of Israel, and strangers to the covenants of promise, having no hope and without God in the world. But now in Christ Jesus you who once were far off have been brought near by the blood of Christ. For he is our peace; in his flesh he has made both groups into one and has broken down the dividing wall, that is, the hostility between us. He has abolished the law with its commandments and ordinances, that he might create in himself one new humanity in place of the two, thus making peace, and might reconcile both groups to God in one body through the cross, thus putting to death that hostility through it."

As the disciples ate and drank with Jesus during His earthly life, we enjoy the most precious table fellowship both with our Lord and His own continually. It is astounding being able to listen to the wisest mortals of all times, to speak to former kings and presidents (those few who were born anew[6]), and to question the greatest redeemed individuals from all throughout history.

Though we do have differences in perspective, we are all forever of one mind with complete doctrinal agreement (something never achieved in the mortal sphere). No longer is there suspicion between brethren, rivalry or envy, or cooled affections. There is no pride or belittling others since each bears so beautifully the divine image. There is no one to sow discord and cause tension in the body, and there are no longer cliques, hidden agendas, insincerity, or the manipulation of others for selfish ends. All quarrels and conflicts were forever settled at the Judgment Seat of Christ. This perfect harmony is part of the unity which is exhibited throughout the entire new heavens and new earth in this one universe united under one Lord for all eternity.

It has been such an enriching experience getting to know the saints from the Bible. Adam is a wonderful person, but he has had to answer the question over and over again "Why did you eat of the forbidden fruit?" His loving, gracious response, given over and over again, was indeed touching. I so enjoyed

---

6. 1 Cor 1:26–29—"Consider your own call, brothers and sisters: not many of you were wise by human standards, not many were powerful, not many were of noble birth. But God chose what is foolish in the world to shame the wise; God chose what is weak in the world to shame the strong; God chose what is low and despised in the world, things that are not, to reduce to nothing things that are, so that no one might boast in the presence of God." Matt 7:13–14—"Enter through the narrow gate; for the gate is wide and the road is easy that leads to destruction, and there are many who take it. For the gate is narrow and the road is hard that leads to life, and there are few who find it."

hearing Noah tell of his experience in preparing for and being preserved through the great flood. It was also awesome hearing Paul explain more fully the epistle to the Romans and learning what he meant by each word and each grammatical construction. I sat for days listening to Isaiah (there really was only one) explain the structure and meaning of his prophecy. It was very enlightening hearing Solomon explain the framework and elaborate figures of speech in the Song of Solomon, explaining exactly what was in his mind throughout the text. I was especially interested in meeting the author of the epistle to the Hebrews and finding out what he had in mind in chapters 6 and 10 when he warned his readers of apostasy. I have also spent many hours conversing with, and being inspired by, other Biblical characters like Abraham, Joseph, Moses, Elijah, Peter, and John. David continues to write such beautiful Psalms and to lead some of the heavenly choirs as they sing music which makes the inhabitants of heaven utterly ecstatic.

We live in a world without disappointments, frustrations, or setbacks. There are no more persecutions, suffering caused by others, or misunderstandings; I have never been offended a single time in this new world. I have never seen another person look despairingly upon me, and I have never heard a bitter or sarcastic remark spoken by anyone.

In the new earth all relationships are rooted in righteousness and holiness; every contact, every experience, every relationship, propels us to greater heights of devotion and godliness and more intimate relationship with our common Lord. As a result, all human friendships have been elevated, made more profound, and far more satisfying than had previously been possible. All of the hindrances to fellowship, all earthly barriers, which were so ubiquitous in the mortal life have been removed so that there is perpetual, undisturbed, and open communion with all the people of God.

It is awesome seeing how the image of God is reflected so sharply and powerfully through the corporate body made up of millions of individual image bearers, each of whom mirrors the likeness of God in a distinct way. And what beauty, what symmetry, harmony, and unimaginable splendor is exuded when those millions of combined images reflect together and more fully the likeness of their common Lord. Heaven is filled with saints each of whom reflects the likeness of God in a unique way so that God's likeness is made more visible through the millions of smaller reflections. There is an endless variety and diversity with the millions of redeemed personalities, with their varying gifts, backgrounds, and personal histories, now transformed and purified from all stain in the glorified state. An absolute unity exists among the many in which the diversities are preserved and allowed to develop so that the whole is enriched and the joy of the parts is heightened.[7]

7. 1 Cor 12: 4–27—"Now there are varieties of gifts, but the same Spirit; and there are varieties of services, but the same Lord; and there are varieties of activities, but it is the same God who activates all of them in everyone. To each is given the manifestation of the Spirit for the common good. To one is given through the Spirit the utterance of wisdom, and to another the utterance of knowledge according to the same Spirit, to another faith by the same Spirit, to another gifts of healing by the one Spirit, to another the working of miracles, to another prophecy, to another the discernment of spirits, to another various kinds of tongues, to another the interpretation of tongues. All these are activated by one and the same Spirit, who allots to each one individually just as the Spirit chooses. For just as the body is one and has many members, and all the members of the body, though many, are one body, so it is with Christ. For in the one Spirit we were all baptized into one body—Jews or Greeks, slaves or free—and we were all made to drink of one Spirit. Indeed, the body does not consist of one member but of many. If the foot would say, 'Because I am not a hand, I do not belong to the body,' that would not make it any less a part of the body. And if the ear would say, 'Because I am not an eye, I do not belong to the body,' that would not make it any

Heaven is a society of redeemed and glorified people with a huge population each of whom shares the same salvation and each of whom, even the least of the saints, has a divinely-appointed role and place in which he or she contributes to the whole by adding light, truth, or happiness. Each learns from the knowledge, wisdom, and experience of his fellow saints. Furthermore, the deepest appreciation is expressed for parents, contributors, pastors, and friends; in fact, no aid, assistance, or encouragement received from other believers is forgotten. The scars and sufferings of the godly are also remembered with sympathy and deepest appreciation.

The perfect love which exists between persons means that there is a common inheritance, that all things are held in common with a spirit of mutuality and reciprocity.[8] The gift

---

less a part of the body. If the whole body were an eye, where would the hearing be? If the whole body were hearing, where would the sense of smell be? But as it is, God arranged the members in the body, each one of them, as he chose. If all were a single member, where would the body be? As it is, there are many members, yet one body. The eye cannot say to the hand, 'I have no need of you,' nor again the head to the feet, 'I have no need of you.' On the contrary, the members of the body that seem to be weaker are indispensable, and those members of the body that we think less honorable we clothe with greater honor, and our less respectable members are treated with greater respect; whereas our more respectable members do not need this. But God has so arranged the body, giving the greater honor to the inferior member, that there may be no dissension within the body, but the members may have the same care for one another. If one member suffers, all suffer together with it; if one member is honored, all rejoice together with it. Now you are the body of Christ and individually members of it."

8. Eph 4:11–16—"The gifts he gave were that some would be apostles, some prophets, some evangelists, some pastors and teachers, to equip the saints for the work of ministry, for building up the body of Christ, until all of us come to the unity of the faith and of the knowledge of the Son of God, to maturity, to the measure of the full stature of Christ. We must

of heaven is one which is received, enjoyed, and fully shared by all. In fact the glory of one member is considered the glory of all. This attitude of rejoicing in the wealth and joy of one another causes the capital of transcendent joy and happiness, the property of all, to increase exponentially. The inhabitants of this city are not merely guests, but they dwell as members of the Master's house, His very family. The treasures of heaven, as well as its unending joys, are shared by all. How amazing finding the satisfactions provided by the Creator to have been tailored so perfectly to fit our individual needs and at the same time to contribute so substantially to the fullness of the redeemed community. Now the great inexhaustible treasures of heaven are the common property of all. Instead of jealousy and envy, the bliss of one is the bliss of the whole redeemed community.

---

no longer be children, tossed to and fro and blown about by every wind of doctrine, by people's trickery, by their craftiness in deceitful scheming. But speaking the truth in love, we must grow up in every way into him who is the head, into Christ, from whom the whole body, joined and knit together by every ligament with which it is equipped, as each part is working properly, promotes the body's growth in building itself up in love."

9

Activities Here

Eternity

Dear _____,

In this eternal world there is intense activity as the redeemed serve God continually without intermission. They are engaged in many duties, important occupations, and essential functions that are both edifying and delightful and, most important of all, bring glory to God.[1] The life in God's eternal presence never grows old; in fact, every moment is satisfying, thrilling and exciting. What God made new[2] continues to maintain the quality of newness about it. There is certainly great earnestness

---

1. Matt 24: 45–47—"Who then is the faithful and wise slave, whom his master has put in charge of his household, to give the other slaves their allowance of food at the proper time? Blessed is that slave whom his master will find at work when he arrives. Truly I tell you, he will put that one in charge of all his possessions." Matt 25:21—"His master said to him, 'Well done, good and trustworthy slave; you have been trustworthy in a few things, I will put you in charge of many things; enter into the joy of your master.'" Luke 19:17—"He said to him, 'Well done, good slave! Because you have been trustworthy in a very small thing, take charge of ten cities.'"

2. Rev 21:5—"And the one who was seated on the throne said, 'See, I am making all things new.' Also he said, 'Write this, for these words are trustworthy and true.'"

and contemplation of the things of God and fellowship with the whole company of the redeemed. But our total preoccupation is with God Himself,[3] so that the knowledge of Him takes absolute priority over everything else.

The activity which is of greatest concern and the most continuous duration is that of worship of the Triune God. Offering unending worship of God, which is spontaneous and unrestricted, is our highest activity, the first priority of heaven. In a real sense every creaturely activity relates to God and is an act of worship, part of our priestly service to Him. But there is a special adoration of God in which His perfections are adored and His works are remembered with thanksgiving in both prayer and meditation.[4] God is worshiped in spirit and in truth[5] and in

---

3. Ps 73:25—"Whom have I in heaven but you? And there is nothing on earth that I desire other than you." 2 Cor 5:8—"Yes, we do have confidence, and we would rather be away from the body and at home with the Lord." John 17:24—"Father, I desire that those also, whom you have given me, may be with me where I am, to see my glory, which you have given me because you loved me before the foundation of the world."

4. Ps 27:4—"One thing I asked of the Lord, that will I seek after: to live in the house of the Lord all the days of my life, to behold the beauty of the Lord, and to inquire in his temple." Ps 48:9—"We ponder your steadfast love, O God, in the midst of your temple." Ps 96:7–9—"Ascribe to the Lord, O families of the peoples, ascribe to the Lord glory and strength. Ascribe to the Lord the glory due his name; bring an offering, and come into his courts. Worship the Lord in holy splendor; tremble before him, all the earth." 1 Pet 2:5—"[L]ike living stones, let yourselves be built into a spiritual house, to be a holy priesthood, to offer spiritual sacrifices acceptable to God through Jesus Christ."

5. John 4:23–24—"But the hour is coming, and is now here, when the true worshipers will worship the Father in spirit and truth, for the Father seeks such as these to worship him. God is spirit, and those who worship him must worship in spirit and truth."

the beauty of holiness[6] here in heaven. The Psalms are now given their perfect fulfillment in this sublime worship. What an awesome sight seeing saints, apostles, martyrs, and the most exalted angels all bowing in lowliness before the absolute Sovereign of the universe, forming the largest choir ever assembled, with all its members spontaneously singing praise from an overflowing heart and exalting God's majesty and power, with the confession that whatever is offered is inadequate for this eternal Sovereign.[7] This worship arises as a natural response to the greatness of God's being and actions. This worship is sheer pleasure, a delight superseding any earthly pleasures, more exhilarating than anything ever experienced in the mortal life.

The music of heaven far surpasses all of the music of the mortal order with its purity, sincerity, harmony, and unity. When the ransomed sing the praises of their Creator and Redeemer with glorified voices in the very presence of their Savior, even the angels marvel at the beauty, depth, and profundity of the song of worship. It is as though the thresholds of heaven shake and rock[8] when the great universal congregation made up of men and women from all peoples, tongues, tribes, and nations sing,

6. Ps 29:2—"Ascribe to the Lord the glory of his name; worship the Lord in holy splendor."

7. 1 Kgs 8:27—"But will God indeed dwell on the earth? Even heaven and the highest heaven cannot contain you, much less this house that I have built!" Ps 116:12–13—"What shall I return to the Lord for all his bounty to me? I will lift up the cup of salvation and call on the name of the Lord." Rom 11:33–36—"O the depth of the riches and wisdom and knowledge of God! How unsearchable are his judgments and how inscrutable his ways! 'For who has known the mind of the Lord? Or who has been his counselor?' 'Or who has given a gift to him, to receive a gift in return?' For from him and through him and to him are all things. To him be the glory forever. Amen."

8. Isa 6:3–4—"And one called to another and said: 'Holy, holy, holy is the Lord of hosts; the whole earth is full of his glory.' The pivots on the

> You are worthy, our Lord and God, to receive glory and honor and power, for you created all things, and by your will they existed and were created.[9]
>
> You are worthy to take the scroll and to open its seals, for you were slaughtered and by your blood you ransomed for God saints from every tribe and language and people and nation; you have made them to be a kingdom and priests serving our God, and they will reign on earth.[10]
>
> Worthy is the Lamb that was slaughtered to receive power and wealth and wisdom and might and honor and glory and blessing![11]
>
> To the one seated on the throne and to the Lamb be blessing and honor and glory and might forever and ever![12]

God in His grace even allows us to have visions in which we view the great events of the Bible. I must have seen the cross and resurrection of the Savior ten thousand times—I just cannot get over the reality of what He did as my personal substitute and representative. I also love watching the Savior's miracles of healing, casting out demons, controlling nature, and raising the dead. We also get to see other events like the Flood, the Exodus, and Pentecost as well as seeing again the destruction of the former universe and the recreation of the heavens and the earth.

---

thresholds shook at the voices of those who called, and the house filled with smoke."

9. Rev 4:11.
10. Rev 5:9–10.
11. Rev 5:10–12.
12. Rev 5:13.

In fulfillment of the original creation mandate[13] we are continually employed using the talents and gifts bequeathed individually to us by our all-wise and loving Creator (some of which were inconceivable in the former world) in ways which are creative and show forth His glory. The absence of sin and the full presence of the Spirit allow the powers of the mind to be developed and the emotions of the heart to be expressed in ways which were previously not possible. This new world is filled with intellectual, cultural, and artistic advancements which make all achievements in the former world seem juvenile. We are privileged to be able to serve our God[14] in so many different ways; each is so delightful that it would be erroneous to call it "work" (this is a word from the former world which has no counterpart in the new heavens and the new earth). What we do is without sweat, weariness, or fear of failure, error, or disobedience to God. It is done as worship and service to God and is thus a joy and a delight, especially since what we do is particularly adapted to our own distinctive tastes, abilities, and desires. Serving God without intermission is perfect freedom and the highest glory which is possible for a human being. We also labor in an atmosphere where competition does not exist; rather, each has great joy in contributing to the growth and understanding of

13. Gen 1:26–28—"Then God said, 'Let us make humankind in our image, according to our likeness; and let them have dominion over the fish of the sea, and over the birds of the air, and over the cattle, and over all the wild animals of the earth, and over every creeping thing that creeps upon the earth.' So God created humankind in his image, in the image of God he created them; male and female he created them. God blessed them, and God said to them, 'Be fruitful and multiply, and fill the earth and subdue it; and have dominion over the fish of the sea and over the birds of the air and over every living thing that moves upon the earth.'"

14. Rev 7:15—"For this reason they are before the throne of God, and worship him day and night within his temple, and the one who is seated on the throne will shelter them."

the entire community. We rejoice in the products of our neighbor's labors and his creative expression. With our responsibilities and service constituting nothing but pure joy because they are tasks committed to us by God and done for His glory, "work" and pleasure cannot be distinguished. Labor now is in fact rest, and work is pure joy. Desire and fulfillment have become one and the same. We are in this world allowed to finish those tasks which had to be left undone on earth because of lack of time, strength, or ability. All we do is perfectly fulfilling, restful, and deeply satisfying. What an awesome honor it is for God to place us in His service.

We do not labor only as servants, but in the wonder of God's saving grace, we have been made to sit with Christ on His throne and reign with Him.[15] We share His inheritance as our Elder brother.[16] Though I was not born of wealthy or royal parents in the previous life (that fact seems so trivial to me now, not even worth remembering), how amazing to be a joint heir with Jesus Christ and to reign as a priest and king with Him.[17] It was indeed solemn being judged by Christ, declared just, and then

---

15. Rev 3:21—"To the one who conquers I will give a place with me on my throne, just as I myself conquered and sat down with my Father on his throne."

16. Rom 8:16–17—"[I]t is that very Spirit bearing witness with our spirit that we are children of God, and if children, then heirs, heirs of God and joint heirs with Christ—if, in fact, we suffer with him so that we may also be glorified with him." Gal 4:7—"So you are no longer a slave but a child, and if a child then also an heir, through God."

17. Rev 1:6—"[A]nd made us to be a kingdom, priests serving his God and Father, to him be glory and dominion forever and ever. Amen." Rev 5:10—"[Y]ou have made them to be a kingdom and priests serving our God, and they will reign on earth." Rev 20:6—"Blessed and holy are those who share in the first resurrection. Over these the second death has no power, but they will be priests of God and of Christ, and they will reign with him a thousand years."

crowned. But it was truly awesome when He appointed us as judges to share in His judgment of the world and of the angels.[18] When we remember where we were in our lost estate and what we justly deserved from God's wrath, we realize that all eternity will not afford enough time nor opportunity to render sufficient thanksgiving and praise to God for the wonder and the depth of His grace, which has been extended to us.

---

18. 1 Cor 6:2–3—"Do you not know that the saints will judge the world? And if the world is to be judged by you, are you incompetent to try trivial cases? Do you not know that we are to judge angels—to say nothing of ordinary matters?"

10

Implications for the Mortal Life

Eternity

Dear _____,

As I look back on the earthly existence I cannot help but be amazed, that even with the great promises of God concerning eternity and the incomparable invitation to receive forgiveness and eternal life freely though faith in Jesus Christ, how men kept so immersed in their daily vocations, estates, and hobbies that few gave serious attention to the eternal future which most certainly loomed ahead of them[1] and which they should have seen evidenced both in the daily obituary pages[2] and the Second Law of Thermodynamics (the observed principle that the universe was slowly winding down to nothing). Men trained for careers, fine-tuned their portfolios, and laid up as much as they could for their retirement, but omitted preparation for eternity. Many ridiculed those who attempted to proclaim God's truth to them concerning future realities.[3] Even believers who professed

---

1. Matt 24:37–39—"For as the days of Noah were, so will be the coming of the Son of Man. For as in those days before the flood they were eating and drinking, marrying and giving in marriage, until the day Noah entered the ark, and they knew nothing until the flood came and swept them all away, so too will be the coming of the Son of Man."

2. Heb 9:27—"And just as it is appointed for mortals to die once, and after that the judgment."

3. 2 Pet 3:3–4—"First of all you must understand this, that in the last days scoffers will come, scoffing and indulging their own lusts and saying,

to believe what the Bible teaches concerning eternity, often did not live in the light of those truths; there was a dreadful gap between their profession and their possession. Sadly too, some believers had put more stress on designing and defending the most elaborate eschatological charts (none of which was completely accurate) than they had on achieving personal holiness and extending the message of the Gospel.

The first great reality that I would encourage all mortals to consider is their own relationship to the person and work of Jesus Christ. Ultimately and finally all that matters is whether a person is in saving union with Christ by faith—on that question hangs his or her eternal destiny (He is the Way to God, the only Way).[4] The person who is in Christ has his eternal future made secure[5] and needs to realize that every other factor in the mortal world (job, family, finances, friends, etc.) is of comparatively little importance.[6] There is indeed a rest for those in Christ, but

---

'Where is the promise of his coming? For ever since our ancestors died, all things continue as they were from the beginning of creation!'"

4. John 14:6—"Jesus said to him, 'I am the way, and the truth, and the life. No one comes to the Father except through me.'" Acts 4:12—"There is salvation in no one else, for there is no other name under heaven given among mortals by which we must be saved."

5. John 5:24—"Very truly, I tell you, anyone who hears my word and believes him who sent me has eternal life, and does not come under judgment, but has passed from death to life."

6. Matt 6:25–34—"Therefore I tell you, do not worry about your life, what you will eat or what you will drink, or about your body, what you will wear. Is not life more than food, and the body more than clothing? Look at the birds of the air; they neither sow nor reap nor gather into barns, and yet your heavenly Father feeds them. Are you not of more value than they? And can any of you by worrying add a single hour to your span of life? And why do you worry about clothing? Consider the lilies of the field, how they grow; they neither toil nor spin, yet I tell you, even Solomon in all his glory was not clothed like one of these. But if

only for those.[7] The believer need not fear death, as others do, because he has God's promise of His presence in that hour.[8] In fact, at death the one in Christ takes possession of eternal life in a far greater measure than he has known previously.[9] The truth which Scripture proclaims about heaven and about hell ought to motivate the believer to make it his prime directive to see that the message of the Gospel is proclaimed worldwide to all who do not know the Savior; there is no higher necessity or function.[10] More than one angel has said to me, "If I had been given the opportunity of preaching the Gospel to the unsaved,

---

God so clothes the grass of the field, which is alive today and tomorrow is thrown into the oven, will he not much more clothe you—you of little faith? Therefore do not worry, saying, 'What will we eat?' or 'What will we drink?' or 'What will we wear?' For it is the Gentiles who strive for all these things; and indeed your heavenly Father knows that you need all these things. But strive first for the kingdom of God and his righteousness, and all these things will be given to you as well. So do not worry about tomorrow, for tomorrow will bring worries of its own. Today's trouble is enough for today."

7. Heb 4:9–10—"So then, a sabbath rest still remains for the people of God; for those who enter God's rest also cease from their labors as God did from his."

8. Ps 23:4—"Even though I walk through the darkest valley, I fear no evil; for you are with me; your rod and your staff—they comfort me." 1 Cor 15:55–57—"'Where, O death, is your victory? Where, O death, is your sting?' The sting of death is sin, and the power of sin is the law. But thanks be to God, who gives us the victory through our Lord Jesus Christ."

9. Phil 1:21—"For to me, living is Christ and dying is gain."

10. Matt 28:19–20—"Go therefore and make disciples of all nations, baptizing them in the name of the Father and of the Son and of the Holy Spirit, and teaching them to obey everything that I have commanded you. And remember, I am with you always, to the end of the age." 2 Cor 5:11—"Therefore, knowing the fear of the Lord, we try to persuade others. . . ."

I would have spared no effort in such a glorious opportunity of obediently serving the Sovereign Lord."

Although the human mind really "freezes up" (like the computers in the former world) when it tries to fathom the duration of eternity, the matter of the everlasting destinies of human beings is of the utmost significance. Those fleeting moments in the mortal life have eternal consequences—decisions are made in that sphere with which human beings will have to live forever. It is this fact that makes time (in the previous world) of such inestimable worth and value. The Psalmist prayed, "So teach us to count our days that we may gain a wise heart."[11] While the original physical creation faded away, human beings have an eternal existence. I realize now that every person I met or related to in any way, was destined either for judgment or glory, and every contact was an opportunity of propelling them toward one or the other.

Seeing billions of men and women cast alive into the lake of fire was a real epiphany for me. Though there were many theologians and writers in the previous world who insisted that the concept of hell was mythical, "pre-critical," and unworthy of the God manifested in Christ, I believed that there would be such a place, but I had not been deeply moved by its starkness, severity, and awfulness. However, when I heard the terrible screams of the damned and saw the absolutely indescribable look on their faces of shock, terror, vain denial, and absolute despair, when they heard the most dreadful and irrevocable sentence of doom spoken over their heads ("You that are accursed, depart from me into the eternal fire prepared for the devil and his angels"[12]), I realized in a more profound way how much God

---

11. Ps 90:12.
12. Matt 25:41.

hates sin,[13] how it really grosses Him out,[14] and how dreadful the penalty of sin really is.[15] Each sinner would have been better off if he or she could have suffered a billion years for every sin committed rather than having to pay such a great debt to the infinite God throughout all eternity. The reality of hell made me appreciate the infinite value of the Gospel, the great love of God in providing a way of salvation at infinite cost to Himself, and the urgency in the mortal life of calling men to repentance.[16] I wondered what it would be like if it were possible to take one of the lost out of the lake of fire (actually no one ever returns from the lake of fire) and interview him after a million or so years. I could not imagine what the look on the face of such a one would be who was in the midst of eternal destruction, having been cast out of God's gracious presence, and made an object of His all-devouring wrath forever. All I could do was to bow in intense thanksgiving and praise for the Lamb of God who had taken away my sin by offering Himself as the propitiatory sacrifice

---

13. Ps 5:5—"The boastful will not stand before your eyes; you hate all evildoers." Rom 1:18—"For the wrath of God is revealed from heaven against all ungodliness and wickedness of those who by their wickedness suppress the truth."

14. Isa 64:6—"We have all become like one who is unclean, and all our righteous deeds are like a filthy cloth [i.e., menstrual cloth]. We all fade like a leaf, and our iniquities, like the wind, take us away."

15. Rom 6:23—"For the wages of sin is death. . . ." Rev 14:10–11—"[T]hey will also drink the wine of God's wrath, poured unmixed into the cup of his anger, and they will be tormented with fire and sulfur in the presence of the holy angels and in the presence of the Lamb. And the smoke of their torment goes up forever and ever. There is no rest day or night for those who worship the beast and its image and for anyone who receives the mark of its name."

16. 2 Cor 6:2—"For he says, 'At an acceptable time I have listened to you, and on a day of salvation I have helped you.' See, now is the acceptable time; see, now is the day of salvation!"

Implications for the Mortal Life 111

by which God's wrath, directed now so powerfully against the unsaved, had been forever turned away from me.[17]

These experiences impressed heavily on me the all-importance of man's spiritual dimension. I came to realize that man is a spiritual being who has a temporary physical existence in the mortal sphere with a life that is capable of being either invested for God's glory or wasted, with eternal consequences in both cases. Nothing is more important for man than setting as his goal the glory of God which is the highest end of all things,[18] and the salvation of souls, which makes the angels, rejoice.[19] Since all things are for Christ, his favor is better than life itself. The one whose existence is Christ-centered is in touch with the true order and purpose of the cosmos.[20] The one whose life is

---

17. I John 2:2—"[A]nd He is the propitiation for our sins . . ." (KJV). Isa 53:5—"But he was wounded for our transgressions, crushed for our iniquities; upon him was the punishment that made us whole, and by his bruises we are healed."

18. Ps 113:4—"The Lord is high above all nations, and his glory is above the heavens." Rom 11:36—"For from him and through him and to him are all things. To him be the glory forever. Amen." Col 1:16—"[F]or in him all things in heaven and on earth were created, things visible and invisible, whether thrones or dominions or rulers or powers—all things have been created through him and for him."

19. Luke 15:7—"Just so, I tell you, there will be more joy in heaven over one sinner who repents than over ninetynine righteous persons who need no repentance."

20. Col 1:17–20—"He himself is before all things, and in him all things hold together. He is the head of the body, the church; he is the beginning, the firstborn from the dead, so that he might come to have first place in everything. For in him all the fullness of God was pleased to dwell, and through him God was pleased to reconcile to himself all things, whether on earth or in heaven, by making peace through the blood of his cross."

directed in any other way is following vanity, illusions, and the lies of the evil one.

It is only in the light of eternity that the significance of the mortal life can be rightly understood and appreciated. It is the unseen spiritual world which is the real, the substantial, and lasting reality, not the former earth which was but a passing shadow, though this is an insight which had to be appropriated by faith in the previous existence.[21] The things of the older earth had value only as they promoted and effected possible eternal outcomes. Knowing the reality of the unseen dimension ought to enable mortal believers to realize that there is a divine design and purpose behind everything that happens. It is through the cultivation of this heavenly perspective (setting our minds on things above)[22] that abundant life is demonstrated. When God freed our affections from the temporary order, He produced in us joy[23] and comfort,[24] and brought about sanctification[25] and

---

21. 2 Cor 4:18—"[B]ecause we look not at what can be seen but at what cannot be seen; for what can be seen is temporary, but what cannot be seen is eternal." Heb 11:3—"By faith we understand that the worlds were prepared by the word of God, so that what is seen was made from things that are not visible."

22. Col 3:2—"Set your minds on things that are above, not on things that are on earth. . . ."

23. Luke 6:22–23—"Blessed are you when people hate you, and when they exclude you, revile you, and defame you on account of the Son of Man. Rejoice in that day and leap for joy, for surely your reward is great in heaven. . . ." 1 Pet 1:8—"Although you have not seen him, you love him; and even though you do not see him now, you believe in him and rejoice with an indescribable and glorious joy. . . ."

24. Heb 10:34—"For you had compassion for those who were in prison, and you cheerfully accepted the plundering of your possessions, knowing that you yourselves possessed something better and more lasting."

25. 1 John 3:2–3—"Beloved, we are God's children now; what we will be has not yet been revealed. What we do know is this: when he is

perseverance, as well as hope and anticipation.[26] I learned that life in the former world was a pilgrimage, and I had been a stranger in a foreign land until the Master called me home.[27]

Scripture often warned men and women not to attempt to make the temporary world their permanent home[28] because it is only sinners who have their portion in the mortal life.[29] I perceive so much more clearly now in eternity that while the former world was the greatest hell that I ever endured, it was the greatest heaven that most people ever experienced. I regret how much of my time and energy was unnecessarily devoted to so many earthly matters with their transient glitter and deceitful seductions. How faintly I perceived that the cares of the world

---

revealed, we will be like him, for we will see him as he is. And all who have this hope in him purify themselves, just as he is pure."

26. Phil 3:20–21—"But our citizenship is in heaven, and it is from there that we are expecting a Savior, the Lord Jesus Christ. He will transform the body of our humiliation that it may be conformed to the body of his glory, by the power that also enables him to make all things subject to himself."

27. 1 Pet 2:11—"Beloved, I urge you as aliens and exiles to abstain from the desires of the flesh that wage war against the soul." Heb 11:14–16—"[F]or people who speak in this way make it clear that they are seeking a homeland. If they had been thinking of the land that they had left behind, they would have had opportunity to return. But as it is, they desire a better country, that is, a heavenly one. Therefore God is not ashamed to be called their God; indeed, he has prepared a city for them."

28. Matt 6:19–21—"Do not store up for yourselves treasures on earth, where moth and rust consume and where thieves break in and steal; but store up for yourselves treasures in heaven, where neither moth nor rust consumes and where thieves do not break in and steal. For where your treasure is, there your heart will be also."

29. Ps 17:14—"[F]rom mortals whose portion in life is in this world . . ."

were a deadly snare.[30] Those who worshiped idols were the true deviants who were woefully and shamefully out of touch with reality.[31] I realize now that those who refused to prepare for eternity, but fixed their minds only on the present world, were the escapists, following passing shadows. When men lost sight of eternity, how dull and worldly they became; they did not praise God and lost the comfort and peace which comes from faith in Him. They lived under the tyranny of disease and death, in a world which was groaning to be delivered[32]; they were subject to vanity and bitter servitude,[33] rather than the sweet yoke of Christ.[34]

---

30. Luke 21:34—"Be on guard so that your hearts are not weighed down with dissipation and drunkenness and the worries of this life, and that day catch you unexpectedly. . . ." Mark 4:19—"[B]ut the cares of the world, and the lure of wealth, and the desire for other things come in and choke the word, and it yields nothing."

31. Ps 115:4–8—"Their idols are silver and gold, the work of human hands. They have mouths, but do not speak; eyes, but do not see. They have ears, but do not hear; noses, but do not smell. They have hands, but do not feel; feet, but do not walk; they make no sound in their throats. Those who make them are like them; so are all who trust in them." 1 Cor 8:4—"Hence, as to the eating of food offered to idols, we know that 'no idol in the world really exists,' and that 'there is no God but one.'"

32. Rom 8:21–22—"[T]hat the creation itself will be set free from its bondage to decay and will obtain the freedom of the glory of the children of God. We know that the whole creation has been groaning in labor pains until now. . . ."

33. John 8:34—"Jesus answered them, 'Very truly, I tell you, everyone who commits sin is a slave to sin.'" Rom 8:2—"For the law of the Spirit of life in Christ Jesus has set you free from the law of sin and of death."

34. Matt 11:29–30—"Take my yoke upon you, and learn from me; for I am gentle and humble in heart, and you will find rest for your souls. For my yoke is easy, and my burden is light."

Implications for the Mortal Life 115

God used the former earth as His training ground for eternity. It was fitting in His eyes for the human nature to be disciplined and ripened for its transformation into the image of the risen Christ. Through the varied experiences of the mortal life, some of which were painful and difficult, God skillfully prepared us for heaven and created within us an appetite and a longing for the great satisfactions He would provide in the eternal world. From eternity we understand more of His wisdom and power in delicately tailoring our specific circumstances throughout our entire lives to make us just what He wanted us to be, to have those capacities which He wanted us to have, and to make us show forth with greater clarity and brilliance His own likeness. Our struggles made us appreciate in a unique way the moral perfection graciously granted to us at glorification. In the former existence we were like caterpillars waiting for the beauty and glory of the next stage; our bodies were like temporary tents waiting for the eternal home.[35] Where we once experienced the glory of grace in its embryonic form, now we live in total atmosphere of grace in its most glorious manifestation.[36]

I came to realize how precious my prayers had been to God.[37] My prayerlessness had been an expression of unbelief in

---

35. Rom 8:23—"[A]nd not only the creation, but we ourselves, who have the first fruits of the Spirit, groan inwardly while we wait for adoption, the redemption of our bodies." 2 Cor 5:1–4—"For we know that if the earthly tent we live in is destroyed, we have a building from God, a house not made with hands, eternal in the heavens. For in this tent we groan, longing to be clothed with our heavenly dwelling—if indeed, when we have taken it off we will not be found naked. For while we are still in this tent, we groan under our burden, because we wish not to be unclothed but to be further clothed, so that what is mortal may be swallowed up by life."

36. Eph 2:7—"[S]o that in the ages to come he might show the immeasurable riches of his grace in kindness toward us in Christ Jesus."

37. Rev 5:8—"When he had taken the scroll, the four living creatures and the twentyfour elders fell before the Lamb, each holding a harp and

God's goodness and providential care for me, a real insult to Him. How merciful He had been to hear and respond to my feeble petitions; even when He did not answer as I requested and would have desired, it was because in His omniscience and love He knew that what I wanted would have been detrimental to my eternal well-being and not in keeping with His sovereign purposes for me. He had even provided the Holy Spirit to intercede for me in the light of my weakness and ignorance[38] and provided the Great High Priest to make intercession for me in heaven.[39] I saw how God treasured my adoration and praise to Him[40] though they seemed so inadequate and weak during my mortal life.

In the former world our understanding of the workings of divine providence and saving grace was so feeble, though we perceived a power, a wisdom, and a majesty in all of God's

---

golden bowls full of incense, which are the prayers of the saints." Rev 8:3–4—"Another angel with a golden censer came and stood at the altar; he was given a great quantity of incense to offer with the prayers of all the saints on the golden altar that is before the throne. And the smoke of the incense, with the prayers of the saints, rose before God from the hand of the angel."

38. Rom 8:26–27—"Likewise the Spirit helps us in our weakness; for we do not know how to pray as we ought, but that very Spirit intercedes with sighs too deep for words. And God, who searches the heart, knows what is the mind of the Spirit, because the Spirit intercedes for the saints according to the will of God."

39. Heb 7:25—"Consequently he is able for all time to save those who approach God through him, since he always lives to make intercession for them."

40. Ps 100:4—"Enter his gates with thanksgiving, and his courts with praise. Give thanks to him, bless his name." John 4:23—"But the hour is coming, and is now here, when the true worshipers will worship the Father in spirit and truth, for the Father seeks such as these to worship him."

actions. We now realize how much God was teaching the enormous angelic host though His providential and gracious dealings with His own.[41] We recognize much more clearly how He was glorified though the faithfulness and perseverance of His saints in their dark and difficult trials as Job's experience demonstrated (God was immensely glorified when Satan had "to eat crow" and was laughed out of heaven).[42] But I also remember times that I doubted God's goodness and wisdom in His ordering of my personal world and realize how absolutely out of place my arrogance was (I was acting as though I had greater wisdom than omniscience).

It was through our sufferings that God especially prepared us for eternity. The sufferings of the former world were totally dwarfed into insignificance by the glory which God's people share in eternity.[43] But so often it took the pains and the hurts of the mortal world to lift our hearts heavenward and to create within us the anticipation of the eternal world. How gracious God was in not allowing us to become too comfortable in the former world. Afflictions kept us from absorption in the temporal world and seeking ultimate rest within it. In fact it was in our deepest setbacks and afflictions that we were made to appreciate

41. Eph 3:8–10—"[T]his grace was given to me to bring to the Gentiles the news of the boundless riches of Christ, and to make everyone see—what is the plan of the mystery hidden for ages in—God who created all things; so that through the church the wisdom of God in its rich variety might now be made known to the rulers and authorities in the heavenly places."

42. Job 1:7–12; 2:3–6; 2:10.

43. Rom 8:18—"I consider that the sufferings of this present time are not worth comparing with the glory about to be revealed to us." 2 Cor 4:17–19—"For this slight momentary affliction is preparing us for an eternal weight of glory beyond all measure because we look not at what can be seen but at what cannot be seen; for what can be seen is temporary, but what cannot be seen is eternal."

the rest and relief that heaven affords.[44] Suffering caused us to meditate on the nature of the resurrection body. We discovered that death and suffering were the gateway to eternal joy. It was truly astounding seeing God's great pleasure in honoring and rewarding the battle-tested soldiers, the triumphant sufferers, the faithful martyrs, and the men and women who had stood the test no matter what afflictions the evil one had been allowed to put them through.[45] The way of faithfulness in duty and testimony proved to be the way of joy and satisfaction.

As heavenly-mindedness was engendered we began to feel more and more out of place in the temporal world. When we were regenerated, we were made new creatures in Christ[46]; the same Creator remade us who later remade the entire cosmos.[47]

44. 1 Pet 1:6–9—"In this you rejoice, even if now for a little while you have had to suffer various trials, so that the genuineness of your faith—being more precious than gold that, though perishable, is tested by fire—may be found to result in praise and glory and honor when Jesus Christ is revealed. Although you have not seen him, you love him; and even though you do not see him now, you believe in him and rejoice with an indescribable and glorious joy, for you are receiving the outcome of your faith, the salvation of your souls." 2 Cor 12:9–10—"[B]ut he said to me, 'My grace is sufficient for you, for power is made perfect in weakness.' So, I will boast all the more gladly of my weaknesses, so that the power of Christ may dwell in me. Therefore I am content with weaknesses, insults, hardships, persecutions, and calamities for the sake of Christ; for whenever I am weak, then I am strong."

45. Jas 1:2–4—"My brothers and sisters, whenever you face trials of any kind, consider it nothing but joy, because you know that the testing of your faith produces endurance; and let endurance have its full effect, so that you may be mature and complete, lacking in nothing." James 1:12—"Blessed is anyone who endures temptation. Such a one has stood the test and will receive the crown of life that the Lord has promised to those who love him."

46. 2 Cor 5:17—"So if anyone is in Christ, there is a new creation: everything old has passed away; see, everything has become new!"

47. Rev 21:1—"Then I saw a new heaven and a new earth. . . ." Rev

After this new birth there was a sense in which we became "misfits" in the older world; it was no longer our home.[48] The "new creation" within us longed eagerly for the new heavens and the new earth of which it was already a part and for which we were being fashioned. The earthly satisfaction was displaced by a new heavenly longing.[49] Our lives were called to reflect in the temporal sphere the values and priorities of eternity rather than the corrupted ideals and patterns of the fallen world around us; we were the first fruits of His new creation[50] (I regret that all too often my life reflected the fallen world rather than the new heavens and the new earth). Those around us ought to have detected the ambience of heaven in the way we spoke and acted.[51] We were called upon by faith to look forward to the glorious return of our Savior and Lord[52] and to the glory of heaven in His pres-

---

21:5—"And the one who was seated on the throne said, 'See, I am making all things new.' Also he said, 'Write this, for these words are trustworthy and true.'"

48. Heb 11:13–14—"All of these died in faith without having received the promises, but from a distance they saw and greeted them. They confessed that they were strangers and foreigners on the earth, for people who speak in this way make it clear that they are seeking a homeland."

49. Psa 84:1–2—"My soul longs, indeed it faints for the courts of the Lord; my heart and my flesh sing for joy to the living God." Rom 8:23—see note 35.

50. Jas 1:18—"In fulfillment of his own purpose he gave us birth by the word of truth, so that we would become a kind of first fruits of his creatures." Rev 14:4—"They have been redeemed from humankind as first fruits for God and the Lamb. . . ."

51. Matt 5:16—"In the same way, let your light shine before others, so that they may see your good works and give glory to your Father in heaven." 1 Pet 2:12—"Conduct yourselves honorably among the Gentiles, so that, though they malign you as evildoers, they may see your honorable deeds and glorify God when he comes to judge."

52. 2 Pet 3:12—"waiting for and hastening the coming of the day

ence. Everything that is truly precious to us was housed securely in the heavenly world to come, so we were exhorted to set our affections on things above.[53] Such a passionate desire for heaven revealed the true place of our citizenship, our sincerity, and the reality of the working of grace in our hearts. Such a longing also proved our love for God, enabled us to love one another more deeply, and prevented us from becoming self-indulgent and self-centered.[54]

The hope of heaven also meant that we had to purify ourselves.[55] God's preserving grace made us active and diligent in using the means of grace to further our sanctification and to "hold on" to the profession of faith, which we had made.[56] We had to be serious in the pursuit of holiness,[57] in the exercise

---

of God." 2 Tim 4:8—"From now on there is reserved for me the crown of righteousness, which the Lord, the righteous judge, will give me on that day, and not only to me but also to all who have longed for his appearing."

53. Col 3:2—"Set your minds on things that are above, not on things that are on earth. . . ."

54. 2 Pet 3:13–14—"But, in accordance with his promise, we wait for new heavens and a new earth, where righteousness is at home. Therefore, beloved, while you are waiting for these things, strive to be found by him at peace, without spot or blemish. . . ."

55. I John 3:3—"And all who have this hope in him purify themselves, just as he is pure."

56. Heb 3:6—"Christ, however, was faithful over God's house as a son, and we are his house if we hold firm the confidence and the pride that belong to hope." Heb 6:18—"[S]o that through two unchangeable things, in which it is impossible that God would prove false, we who have taken refuge might be strongly encouraged to seize the hope set before us." Heb 10:23—"Let us hold fast to the confession of our hope without wavering, for he who has promised is faithful."

57. Heb 12:14—"Pursue after peace with all men, and after the sanctification without which no one will see the Lord."

of self examination,[58] and in keeping ourselves from the defiling influences of the surrounding world.[59] The very thought of heaven led inevitably to the quest for holiness; the heart which was focused on heaven was preserved from giving in to the temptations of the world, the devil, and the flesh. The realization that in heaven there would be no pride, carnal indulgence, envy, anger, covetousness, and self-exaltation ought to motivate the Christian to flee from all such practices and attitudes. It is unthinkable for one who is defiled in body and soul to consider being in the presence of the holy angels and the glorified saints, and even less so in the presence of the God who is infinitely and absolutely holy. How sobering to think of being ushered unexpectedly into heaven itself while covered with shame and defilement. The best fortification against temptation was having the affections thoroughly absorbed by and immersed in the superior and ennobling delights of the heavenly realm.[60]

---

58. 1 Cor 11:28—"Examine yourselves, and only then eat of the bread and drink of the cup." 2 Cor 13:5—"Examine yourselves to see whether you are living in the faith. Test yourselves. Do you not realize that Jesus Christ is in you?—unless, indeed, you fail to meet the test!"

59. 2 Cor 6:17—"Therefore come out from them, and be separate from them, says the Lord, and touch nothing unclean; then I will welcome you, and I will be your father, and you shall be my sons and daughters, says the Lord Almighty." Jude 23—"And others save with fear, pulling them out of the fire; hating even the garment spotted by the flesh" (KJV).

60. Ps 119:10–11—"With my whole heart I seek you; do not let me stray from your commandments. I treasure your word in my heart, so that I may not sin against you. . . ." Phil 3:12–14—"Not that I have already obtained this or have already reached the goal; but I press on to make it my own, because Christ Jesus has made me his own. Beloved, I do not consider that I have made it my own; but this one thing I do: forgetting what lies behind and straining forward to what lies ahead, I press on toward the goal for the prize of the heavenly call of God in Christ Jesus."

One of the angels commented to me, "Did you not understand while you were in the mortal sphere the powerful promises that God had give to those in Christ? You had the testimony of the Most High God, whose word is absolute truth,[61] but who even took an oath concerning Christ's high priestly ministry in your behalf.[62] Heaven and earth would pass away before His promise would fail.[63] And did you not understand the power He gave you, in sending the Holy Spirit to indwell you and there to manifest that same power that brought Jesus Christ from the dead?"[64]

We were called to walk according to the character and hope of those who had been brought into vital and saving union with Jesus Christ. Such a life involved the cultivation of heavenly ideals, living as a responsible citizen upon the earth while

---

61. 1 Sam 15:29—"Moreover the Glory of Israel will not recant or change his mind; for he is not a mortal, that he should change his mind."

62. Heb 7:21—"This was confirmed with an oath; for others who became priests took their office without an oath, but this one became a priest with an oath, because of the one who said to him, 'The Lord has sworn and will not change his mind, "You are a priest forever. . . ."'"

63. Matt 24:35—"Heaven and earth will pass away, but my words shall not pass away."

64. Eph 1:17–21—"I pray that the God of our Lord Jesus Christ, the Father of glory, may give you a spirit of wisdom and revelation as you come to know him, so that, with the eyes of your heart enlightened, you may know what is the hope to which he has called you, what are the riches of his glorious inheritance among the saints, and what is the immeasurable greatness of his power for us who believe, according to the working of his great power. God put this power to work in Christ when he raised him from the dead and seated him at his right hand in the heavenly places, far above all rule and authority and power and dominion, and above every name that is named, not only in this age but also in the age to come."

investing in what is eternal, walking in the light as saints of God by living in holiness (letting go of sinful habits and all fleshly indulgences),[65] and pursuing the fellowship of the children of God upon the earth.[66] It was a life under the sovereign reign of Christ, with everything focused on pleasing Him and extending His kingdom, with the same zeal expended in doing His will as is put forth by the angels in heaven. When human beings lived with this heavenly perspective, meditating on the glorious wealth reserved for them in heaven, in all its splendor and brilliance, then there was a right perspective in the present, and there was the necessary motivation to shape and transform present behavior and thought patterns. Furthermore when God was contemplated in His majesty and greatness, all else vanished into insignificance; we knew Christ as our friend and refuge, and our capacity for service in the eternal realms was heightened.

Another motivating factor (on the negative side) was the contemplation of the future judgment. As one who has seen the former earth being dissolved with fervent heat,[67] the wicked appearing before the omniscient and absolutely righteous Judge and then justly sentenced to eternal retribution,[68] and Christians

65. 2 Pet 3:11—"Since all these things are to be dissolved in this way, what sort of persons ought you to be in leading lives of holiness and godliness. . . ."

66. Heb 10:25—"[N]ot neglecting to meet together, as is the habit of some, but encouraging one another, and all the more as you see the Day approaching."

67. 2 Pet 3:12—"[W]aiting for and hastening the coming of the day of God, because of which the heavens will be set ablaze and dissolved, and the elements will melt with fire."

68. Rev 20:11–15—"Then I saw a great white throne and the one who sat on it; the earth and the heaven fled from his presence, and no place was found for them. And I saw the dead, great and small, standing before the throne, and books were opened. Also another book was opened, the book of life. And the dead were judged according to their

having their whole lives reviewed before Christ's judgment seat (including how they have treated others),[69] I urge you to live daily in the light of that great day. Use every ounce of energy, every moment of time, every resource to glorify Christ and make Him known upon the earth. Let the Holy Spirit reflect His character though you so that the invisible Christ might be made visible through your actions, deeds, and words.

The heavenly perspective also should be evident in other ways. Instead of building mansions and portfolios on earth where all possessions are stained ("the mammon of unrighteousness") and everyone's physical life is terminal, believers ought to be cheerful givers, using financial resources in the light of the values of eternity.[70] They ought to meditate constantly with their minds set on God and His glorious being and works,[71] making loving Him and delighting in Him the greatest endeavor of their

---

works, as recorded in the books. And the sea gave up the dead that were in it, Death and Hades gave up the dead that were in them, and all were judged according to what they had done. Then Death and Hades were thrown into the lake of fire. This is the second death, the lake of fire; and anyone whose name was not found written in the book of life was thrown into the lake of fire."

69. Rom 14:10—"Why do you pass judgment on your brother or sister? Or you, why do you despise your brother or sister? For we will all stand before the judgment seat of God."

70. Luke 16:9—"And I say unto you, Make to yourselves friends of the mammon of unrighteousness; that, when ye fail, they may receive you into everlasting habitations" (KJV). Matt 6:19–20—"Do not store up for yourselves treasures on earth, where moth and rust consume and where thieves break in and steal; but store up for yourselves treasures in heaven, where neither moth nor rust consumes and where thieves do not break in and steal."

71. Ps 1:2—"[B]ut their delight is in the law of the Lord, and on his law they meditate day and night." Psalm 63:6—"[W]hen I think of you on my bed, and meditate on you in the watches of the night."

lives.[72] They need to mediate on His perfections, particularly His infinite love for them personally (a thought which Satan will constantly try to prevent) and to engage in prayer engendered by meditation.[73] They need to see all tasks from the perspective of heaven and thus make the glory of God their motivation.[74] In this way, their lives will become a vestibule of heaven as they partake of holiness.[75]

While living in a world of corruption and rebellion against God, the believer must glorify His heavenly Lord by subduing the flesh though the empowering grace of Christ.[76] He must cooperate with the indwelling Spirit in bringing about the restoration of the image of God within him. In this work of sanctification he will show forth the wonder of God's grace to a world

---

72. Ps 37:4—"Take delight in the Lord, and he will give you the desires of your heart." Ps 31:23—"Love the Lord, all you his saints. . . ." Deut 6:5—"You shall love the Lord your God with all your heart, and with all your soul, and with all your might."

73. 1 Chr 16:28—"Ascribe to the Lord, O families of the peoples, ascribe to the Lord glory and strength. Ascribe to the Lord the glory due his name; bring an offering, and come before him. Worship the Lord in holy splendor." Ps 103:1—"Bless the Lord, O my soul, and all that is within me, bless his holy name." Ps 103:8—"The Lord is merciful and gracious, slow to anger and abounding in steadfast love." Ps 104:1—"Bless the Lord, O my soul. O Lord my God, you are very great. You are clothed with honor and majesty."

74. 1 Cor 10:31—"So, whether you eat or drink, or whatever you do, do everything for the glory of God."

75. Ps 93:5—"Your decrees are very sure; holiness befits your house, O Lord, forevermore."

76. Gal 5:24—"And those who belong to Christ Jesus have crucified the flesh with its passions and desires." Rom 8:13 —"[F]or if you live according to the flesh, you will die; but if by the Spirit you put to death the deeds of the body, you will live."

drowning in shame and wickedness.[77] The progress in holiness, with the daily renewing in the inner man[78] and strengthening the reign of Christ in the soul,[79] will prepare the believer for eternity and produce true comfort and assurance within his own heart.[80]

As the believer loves God supremely he will also grow in love for fellow believers[81] who bear the image of God by cre-

---

77. Eph 2:8–10—"For by grace you have been saved through faith; and that not of yourselves, it is the gift of God; not as a result of works, that no one should boast. For we are His workmanship, created in Christ Jesus for good works, which God prepared beforehand, that we should walk in them." 1 Cor 2:15–16—"For we are the aroma of Christ to God among those who are being saved and among those who are perishing; to the one a fragrance from death to death, to the other a fragrance from life to life. Who is sufficient for these things?"

78. 2 Cor 4:16—"So we do not lose heart. Even though our outer nature is wasting away, our inner nature is being renewed day by day." Rom 12:2—"Do not be conformed to this world, but be transformed by the renewing of your minds, so that you may discern what is the will of God—what is good and acceptable and perfect."

79. 2 Cor 10:5—"[A]nd we take every thought captive to obey Christ." Gal 2:20—"[A]nd it is no longer I who live, but it is Christ who lives in me. And the life I now live in the flesh I live by faith in the Son of God, who loved me and gave himself for me."

80. 2 Pet 1:10–11—"Therefore, brothers and sisters, be all the more eager to confirm your call and election, for if you do this, you will never stumble. For in this way, entry into the eternal kingdom of our Lord and Savior Jesus Christ will be richly provided for you."

81. 1 John 4:19–21—"We love because he first loved us. Those who say, 'I love God,' and hate their brothers or sisters, are liars; for those who do not love a brother or sister whom they have seen, cannot love God whom they have not seen. The commandment we have from him is this: those who love God must love their brothers and sisters also."

ation[82] and the image of Christ by recreation.[83] He will see the image of divine glory shining from eternity in saints who are united with Christ and growing in Christlikeness.[84] He will appreciate and serve those who will be his companions and fellow worshipers throughout all eternity.[85]

I hope that these thoughts will encourage you in your pilgrimage in the mortal sphere, arouse hope and confident expectation within you, and cause you to groan even more for the glorious consummation of salvation which God has for His children. May you truly become what you already are in Christ and will most certainly be in Him as I am now.

---

82. Gen 1:27—"So God created humankind in his image, in the image of God he created them; male and female he created them."

83. Eph 4:24—"[A]nd to clothe yourselves with the new self, created according to the likeness of God in true righteousness and holiness." Col 3:10—"[A]nd have clothed yourselves with the new self, which is being renewed in knowledge according to the image of its creator."

84. 1 Thess 2:19–20—"For what is our hope or joy or crown of boasting before our Lord Jesus at his coming? Is it not you? Yes, you are our glory and joy!" 1 Pet 4:14—"If you are reviled for the name of Christ, you are blessed, because the spirit of glory, which is the Spirit of God, is resting on you." 2 Cor 3:18—"And all of us, with unveiled faces, seeing the glory of the Lord as though reflected in a mirror, are being transformed into the same image from one degree of glory to another; for this comes from the Lord, the Spirit."

85. John 13:14—"And all of us, with unveiled faces, seeing the glory of the Lord as though reflected in a mirror, are being transformed into the same image from one degree of glory to another; for this comes from the Lord, the Spirit." Gal 5:13—"[B]ut through love become slaves to one another."

www.ingramcontent.com/pod-product-compliance
Lightning Source LLC
Chambersburg PA
CBHW050833160426
43192CB00010B/2014